Quality Circle Time
in the
Secondary School

A Handbook of Good Practice

JENNY MOSLEY AND MARILYN TEW

David Fulton Publishers
London

David Fulton Publishers Ltd
Ormond House, 26–27 Boswell Street, London WC1N 3JD

First published in Great Britain by David Fulton Publishers 1999
Reprinted 2000

British Library Cataloguing in Publication Data

A catalogue record for this book is available from the British Library

ISBN 1-85346-616-6

Typeset by Kate Williams, Abergavenny
Printed in Great Britain by Bell and Bain Ltd, Glasgow

Contents

Acknowledgements

Thank you to schools

There are wonderful educators out there doing an amazing job in difficult times. The following people have contributed, either through their writing, through working with us or through consultation to our book, and we value their enthusiasm and sheer 'brave-heartedness' in keeping going with 'The Vision'. Their names are:

Caroline Atherton, Behaviour Support School, Cranford Community School, Essex
Ann Boardman, South Essex Health Authority
Mary Bright, Shoeburyness County High School, Essex
Norma-Davis Cox, Tameside Community Care Trust, South Essex
Mac Davison and Wayne Howells, Heads of Year, John of Gaunt School, Trowbridge, Wiltshire
Doreen Cunningham, Deputy Head, St. Thomas More, Elton, London
Sandra Dixon, Head of Year 7, Project Team Leader for Self-Esteem, Maplesden Noakes, Kent
Edith Forrest, Senior Teacher, Behavioural Support Services, Perth
Sue Gray (photography), Dominic Salles, English Teacher, and Tutor, The Commonweal School, Swindon, Wiltshire
John Wells, Lisa Battaglia, Cathy Owen, Rachael Pickering and Harvey Groves, The Headlands School, Swindon, Wiltshire
Miguel Jackson, Educational Psychologist, Rochdale LEA
Douglas Kimber, Head teacher, Maplesden Noakes, Kent
Michael Marland, CBE, Head teacher, Westminster School, London
Gerry Murray, Head teacher, St. Thomas More, Elton, London
Betty Ports, Deputy Head teacher, All Saints School, Weymouth, Dorset
The Ridgeway School, staff and pupils for allowing Marilyn to do her M.Ed. research there, particularly Heather Siebenaller, Head of PSE, and Priscilla Lane, PSE Teacher
Julia Shepperd, Head teacher, Oakfields School, Swindon, Wiltshire
Esther de Burgh-Thomas, SENCO, Highbury Grove School, London
Isobel McFarlane, Guidance and Behavioural Support Teacher, Fife
Urmila Ramakrishna, Kodaikanal International School, India.

New research

Our thanks go especially to Simon Richey of the Calouste Gulbenkian Foundation who has shown enormous interest in our work and supported our application for funding to run a pilot research project on using Quality Circle Time for PSHE in Headland's School, Swindon. Thanks too go to Peter Robinson, Professor of Psychology, University of Bristol, and Carol Tayler, 6ᵗʰ Form Business Studies Teacher, ex-Deputy Head of Yate School, Bristol, who agreed to evaluate this research.

Special thanks

We would also like to thank the following people who, in their own way, have managed to find paths forward for secondary schools. Titus Alexander, founder of Self-Esteem Network who continually seeks ways of supporting our work and helped us to found the charity All Round Success. Margaret Beckett, former SEN Adviser, Education and Cultural Services, Cardiff County Council, for ensuring that we gave a presentation to their secondary head teachers conference. We would also like to thank Moya Brewer, Harrow Support Services, Harrow, who has helped research into the impact of circle time on year 7 pupils and continually supports the development of Quality Circle Time in secondary schools. Jane Earle, Secondary Pupil Behaviour Support Services, Barking & Dagenham, who is a gifted advocate of our work. Nick Peacey, SENJIT Coordinator, Institute of London for continuing to support and organise our workshops for secondary teachers. Sylvia Moore, Head teacher, Francis Coombe School, Watford and Ansar Iqbal, form tutor, were very supportive when we ran our Quality Circle Time conference at Westminster College; they bused in a class of secondary pupils who gave a sensitive circle time presentation to the adults! James Park from Antidote for hosting the conference. Harrow Education Authority has been very supportive of this approach for many years.

Thank you to the illustrator

We are very grateful to Meg Mosley, Jenny's teenage daughter, who contributed the cartoons. Over the years she has driven us both to the edge at times, but thankfully, she has a great respect for Circle Time and its potential.

Just . . . 'Thank you'

Thank you to Alison Foyle for being a very patient and supportive editor. We would also like to thank our families, friends and partners. Being committed to 'The Cause' does undoubtedly put pressure on those that are close to us. We can often have a slightly wild-eyed, frazzled look that isn't very attractive. Getting the balance right between meeting their, our and Circle Time's needs often tips us over into various ditches – but at least we can look up at the stars!

Foreword

We know, from experience and the most thorough and widespread research, that however good the curriculum provision and skilled the teaching, not all pupils benefit fully. Pupils making best use of their schooling depends on their inner consciousness: their self-understanding, self-esteem, relationships with others, and view of the range of possibilities of life. How can a secondary school stimulate and develop, in the majority of pupils, the personal qualities that only a few bring with them? Jenny Mosley's development of the Whole School Quality Circle Time Model offers a practical way forward, one which is realistic, imaginative, sensitive, and above all 'do-able'.

One secondary school head teacher wrote, in response to the training his staff received from the consultancy:

> What you did today was to give us the best possible springboard for this project of self-esteem. The interest and enthusiasm that has been generated in nearly all adults in the school has been infectious. You have opened minds, you have made us revisit our values, and you have inspired many pupils'.

This book will do just that for secondary school staff.

The early and mid-1990s experienced a poor side-effect of the National Curriculum requirements. It was introduced to ensure that no pupil would miss out because his or her school had a gap in the curriculum, as a number admittedly did. However, by over-rigidly focussing on the National Curriculum requirements, many aspects of a school's aims that were not part of the 'subject curriculum' missed out on the same care, formal analysis and planning. Most secondary schools are now considering, extending and re-emphasising the personal part of the overall teaching aims: how do we enable the youngster to understand how to become a student not a child, and to develop the attitude, self-understanding, and ambitious approaches of a successful student and young adult? Whether we call it 'citizenship' or 'PSHE', the personal–social core of secondary schooling needs emphasising, and the child needs to be helped to develop as a student. The listening core of *Quality Circle Time in the Secondary School* makes an invaluable contribution to this.

Teachers I have both worked with and heard from have spontaneously admired and, most importantly, used the Quality Circle Time approach. The procedures devised, trialled and described from the secondary point of view in this book have prompted many secondary teachers to place in their tutorial periods and some lessons clearly established Quality Circle Time sessions, using approaches found in this book. The 'ground rules' in this text are a hugely successful tool for secondary teachers. Teachers at my own school much enjoyed and admired the training sessions in this approach and found the ideas and techniques really practical and inspiring. Circle Time training confirmed my belief as a teacher in the centrality of the emotional curriculum in successful learning in schools and showed me a demonstrably effective method of developing relationships and communication in the classroom.

How to listen and how to learn from listening are the core techniques explored in this book. It plans for that which is too often left to chance. Lord Puttnam has praised the overall scheme, stressing that 'the most appealing aspect of the Quality Circle Time model is this notion of young people being given time explicitly to socialise with each other'. He highlights what can be especially brought out through this approach; 'Delight, wonder, mystery, pity, beauty and pain are to us as important to our understanding of the human experience as anything I could ever be tested on'.

This is not a rigid scheme, but a way of freshly reviewing young people as people, and learning how to help them develop their characters as self-reflective analysers and planners. The examples of how secondary school pupils feel and think evoked in this text demonstrate the link between technique and flexible sensitivity. This is summed up perfectly by a pupil who is quoted in this book as saying 'I think sitting in a circle helps people to feel good about themselves and express their feelings'.

From my experience as a secondary head teacher, a founder of the National Association for Pastoral Care in Education, and a researcher, lecturer and writer on pastoral care in a number of countries, I strongly commend this study of the secondary school use of Quality Circle Time; the pupils really benefit from it and this text helps us all consider its core points and effectively put them into practice.

Michael Marland, CBE
Head teacher of North Westminster Community School, London

How to use this book

When we asked teachers to read the manuscript of this book, they made some very useful suggestions to future readers. One such piece of advice came from a circle-time 'convert' who heard about the strategies during a training session for year 7 tutors and decided to 'have a go'. He has never looked back and is currently using the approach in his subject specialism, English, and with his year 8 tutor group. His advice to readers of this book is to read the sections that appeal to you most, first. For instance, he was not particularly interested in the underlying theory of circle time. He simply wanted to know how to use it. Consequently, he skipped the chapters on the underlying psychology and philosophy and went straight to the chapters on how to run circle time; the games, activities and drama strategies. Other readers, however, liked to know and understand the theoretical framework before they felt safe about launching into any new strategies. Your approach to the book will also depend on whether you are a classroom practitioner who wants to improve your own practice or a manager who is looking at the whole-school system. It is to be hoped that the structure of the book will allow you to mix and match. You may well want to read the information in Parts II and III, 'have a go' at running circle time and then read Parts I and IV in order to find out why it works! That is fine, the individual sections stand alone, but we would advise looking sooner rather than later at Chapter 3 on making a commitment to your own self-esteem and morale, so that you can sustain the energy and motivation needed to continue running successful circles.

Another colleague, who has shown great interest in the progress of this book, has been running support circle sessions for pupils at risk of disaffection. He discovered early on that the name 'circle time' had an adverse effect on the pupils. They associated the name with primary school days and therefore dismissed the process as irrelevant to them now that they were in years 8 and 9. Once the name was changed to 'Interface', exactly the same activities, strategies and processes became acceptable and even desirable!

No matter what your starting point or your focus of interest, the book contains all that you need to know about the 'why' and 'how' of establishing circle time in the classroom and the philosophy and psychology of a whole-school circle-time policy whether you are a:

- **subject specialist**
- **PSE specialist or tutor**
- **head of house**
- **head of year**
- **special needs teacher**
- **behavioural support teacher**
- **educational psychologist**
- **drama specialist.**

Part I

The Context for Circle Time

Supporting behaviour management:

... The Whole School Quality Circle Time Model ... can help improve and maintain high standards of behaviour and discipline.

Page 7, Guidance Notes from DfEE,
Circular No. 10/99, July 1999

1 Introducing Circle Time in secondary schools

Doesn't Circle Time belong in primary schools?

For a number of years now, Circle Time has been a 'buzz' term in primary education and like any new trend it is vulnerable to misuse and abuse. We have heard 'Circle Time' applied to a superficial news round where children sat in a circle and shouted out one-word responses to the class teacher's question about their weekend. Similarly, we heard a recent story of a teacher who felt she had only run a good 'Circle Time' if pupils had been manoeuvred into talking about matters they later wished they had kept private. Such accounts are enough to cause most teachers either to dismiss the process as superficial and meaningless, or to be filled with horror! Those who are reading about this subject for the first time should be reassured that in both the cases cited, the teachers had failed to adhere to the basic ground rules and structures advocated in our particular model of Circle Time.

'That's all very well', I hear secondary teachers say. 'But what has a primary school practice, even a good one, got to do with the secondary school?' The answer is that there is a growing challenge. Many thousands of children who have been involved in circle-time meetings in their primary schooling are entering secondary school. Many of these children have been part of schools that have a whole-school circle-time approach. In regular, weekly circle-time meetings, they have grasped an understanding of the value of the individual and the notion of consultation. As part of a class, they have developed supportive peer relationships, giving and receiving class certificates signed by the rest of the class. They are used to holding positions of responsibility such as 'child of the week' when they become the teacher's right hand person, or a 'buddy' to a younger child. Often they have received specific training for positions of wider responsibility in the school such as 'peer mediators', 'guardian angels', 'playground friends' or school council members. They are used to taking turns and know that they can speak and be heard. They have a clear understanding of the need for rules in a school community and the rewards and sanctions that accompany them. They are used to receiving regular good news about their behaviour and academic progress in the form of stickers, stamps and certificates and are in no doubt as to the expectations of their school. Concepts as esoteric as democracy and citizenship have been experienced through the functioning of their classroom and school environments.

Do young people get such a good deal in secondary school?

Though many will argue that these experiences are not consistently found throughout the primary sector, a significant number of children are entering secondary school from this foundation. Once in secondary school, what happens to these young people? The following questions provide a few indicators:

- **Are the moral values of the school made explicit, displayed and discussed so that pupils have the same clear understanding of expectations in their secondary school as they had in the primary?**
- **Do they encounter teachers who use rewards and punishments in a consistent way? Or do you hear pupils say 'You could be perfect and still not get a merit in his class.'**
- **Do 'middle plodder' pupils also get plenty of rewards and commendations?**
- **Do members of staff frequently offer tangible rewards for moral qualities such as honesty and kindness as well as academic success?**
- **Are pupils consulted about management concerns such as litter, toilet provision, dining hall arrangements etc. and actively involved in formulating school policy?**
- **Do pupils have a timetabled, regular time to speak and be heard which ensures that quiet pupils also receive attention?**
- **Do special needs pupils feel accepted and integrated in the school?**
- **Can pupils become trained to be part of a 'bully patrol'?**
- **Are pupils part of a 'befriending' or 'buddy' system?**

We find that the answer to many of these questions is often a resounding 'No'. For a number of young people as they enter secondary school, they encounter conflicting messages and a system in which they often feel powerless and without a voice. In an age of rising exclusions, school refusal and absenteeism, something must be done to bridge the 'divide' that so often exists between the philosophies of primary and secondary schools in their approaches to personal, social and moral and health education (PSE, PSME, PSHE).

Could Circle Time be the bridge between behaviour management and PSHE?

Many primary schools approach the personal and social development of children in a holistic way. The structure of the school with a single class teacher for the majority of subjects makes it much easier to develop a cohesive approach to PSHE and behaviour. In secondary schools, the curriculum is divided up and subjects grouped by faculty. It is all too easy to view PSHE as another subject occupying a timetabled slot, and not as a process of personal, social development that affects every aspect of a pupil's thinking and behaviour.

The problem with this structural organisation is that it creates a false divide between PSHE and behaviour. In the UK we are currently very concerned about deteriorating behaviour and schools have adopted a range of positive behaviour models. Since the 1970s, we have also developed a great variety of PSHE models. Yet in most secondary schools, approaches to behaviour and PSHE operate with separate policies. It is vital that we recognise that the two are indivisible. Internalising moral values is the key to both policies, and 'relationships' form the bridge between the two. Exploring the relationship between others and ourselves is key to personal and social development and empathy is the quality that needs to be developed. Only if people understand and care about other people's inner worlds will they modify their behaviour.

There's nothing new or does it need saying again?

As long ago as 1989, the Elton Report highlighted the role of positive relationships in the teaching and learning environment.

> To be fully effective . . . teachers need . . . the ability to relate to young people, to encourage them in good behaviour and learning, and to deal calmly but firmly with inappropriate or disruptive behaviour. As a useful shorthand we refer to it in our report as 'group management skills'.
>
> Teachers with good group management skills are able to establish positive relationships with their classes based on mutual respect. They can create a classroom climate in which pupils lose rather than gain popularity with their classmates by causing trouble. . . . Good group managers understand how groups of young people react to each other and to teachers. They also understand and are in full control of their own behaviour.
>
> Establishing good relationships with pupils, encouraging them to learn and to behave well have always been essential parts of a teacher's work. This cannot be achieved by talking at children, but by working with them.
>
> (Elton Report 1989: 67–8)

In many secondary schools, the majority of teachers are tutors and often they are required to deliver the PSHE or pastoral programme as part of their role. As subject specialists, they have a knowledge base and have learned how to plan and deliver lessons, but all too frequently, they have received little or no training in the group management skills essential for teaching PSHE. Consequently, they fall back on delivering information about PSHE issues (e.g. drugs, hygiene, smoking, study skills) without entering into a process that develops relationships and moral values, examines attitudes, cultivates empathy and engenders peer support. Circle Time provides structures and strategies for developing this group process.

You may well be reading this thinking, 'Come on, there is no real problem, young people mostly turn out all right in the end.' Although it may be true that the vast majority of pupils in secondary schools are currently behaving satisfactorily and complete their schooling without undue difficulty, there is a feeling in the teaching profession that behaviour is deteriorating (Taylor 1998). Alongside this, a worrying new trend was highlighted in three comprehensive schools that we recently worked in. Tutors had become so disillusioned with the demands of delivering the pastoral programme that they had 'lobbied' to abandon regular tutorial work. In one of the schools, they now have one half day each half term for PSHE where a key speaker gives a presentation to the whole year group. When one of these schools was asked why it chose this route, a senior member of staff said:

Most staff were fed up trying to deliver the tutorial programme. Senior management then felt that tutor time was being used unproductively causing disruption in lessons that followed. The National Curriculum 'squeezes' the timetable, so we have reduced the tutorial programme to a two-hourly session once a half term.

If this level of teacher discomfort with delivering PSHE became a countrywide trend, the results could have far-reaching repercussions given the close link between PSHE and behaviour.

> Our evidence leads us to conclude that . . . teacher's group management skills are probably the single most important factor in achieving good standards of classroom behaviour . . . Those skills can be taught and learned.   (Elton 1989: 70)

Abandon tutorial time or abandon hope?

Abandoning tutorial work is effectively abandoning teambuilding in the classroom. Once teambuilding goes, it becomes very difficult to create a community of civilised citizens who understand how their behaviour impinges on those around them. For many young people, the tutor time and relationships within the tutor group create the secure family base which they do not get in any other part of their life. Without proactive development of teambuilding in this tutor group, the young people quickly form cliques. They group themselves with people who have similar interests and worldviews, i.e. those who do not present any challenge to the way in which they think and behave. These groups then put names or labels on one another. We have heard subsections of tutor groups call each other the 'keenies', the 'swots', the 'tarts', the 'slappers' etc. If the tutor base does not provide an emotionally safe place for debate, negotiation, discussion and developing empathy, the factions continue. One group 'winds up' another in order to pull the other down and thus establish a moment of perceived superiority. In the absence of deliberate teambuilding, team destruction takes place. Attitudes, behaviour and values go unchallenged and become more entrenched resulting in many pupils feeling afraid to achieve their potential and others choosing to opt out of the school system.

Equally worrying was the result of a quick survey of newly qualified secondary teachers at a recent conference. We discovered that very few had received any training in the skills needed for being a tutor and dealing with the pastoral care and personal, social development of young people. It is not surprising that teachers feel ill equipped to deliver a pastoral programme, yet we cannot afford to abandon tutorial work.

Is PSHE important?

Perhaps the most relevant opinion on PSHE, behaviour, relationships, and the value and importance of a process such as Circle Time belongs to the pupils:

> I feel this Circle Time is a great idea . . . If we have time to just talk and let go of all the things we are holding inside us, without someone breathing down our necks and trying to shut us up, it first calms us down and second we can think better.   (Rishabh, 13 years)

5

It makes you feel that you are not the only person with problems or worries about yourself. It makes you have more self-confidence, more self-esteem because before I felt 'Oh I don't like my face or I wish I could change this' but when you speak about things like that in the circle it makes you realise that other people have the same worries as you and you are not abnormal when you have those thoughts.   (Katy, 12 years)

Crushed by the curriculum?

The National Curriculum lays great emphasis on content and more than ever before, the education system and educators are under pressure to meet national targets. Yet a growing body of knowledge arising from the work of Peter Salovey, Howard Gardner and others, highlighted in Daniel Goleman's book *Emotional Intelligence* (1996), points towards the importance of understanding and managing emotions in the learning process. A recent survey carried out by the Mental Health Foundation on promoting children and young people's mental health (*The Big Picture*, February 1999) developed a new definition of children's mental health based on that of the Health Advisory Service.

Children who are mentally healthy will have the ability to:

- develop psychologically, emotionally, creatively, intellectually and spiritually
- initiate, develop and sustain mutually satisfying personal relationships
- use and enjoy solitude
- become aware of others and empathise with them
- play and learn
- develop a sense of right and wrong
- face problems and setbacks and learn form them in ways appropriate for that child's age.   (ibid.: 7)

The report noted in its summary that:

The number of British children experiencing mental ill health has increased since the 1940s to an estimated one in five. Mental health problems in children and young people will continue to increase unless there is a coherent and holistic programme implemented to develop the emotional and mental health of our children ... Emotionally literate children are less likely to experience mental health problems and, if they develop them, are less likely to suffer long term. Emotional literacy is derived from a combination of parents, schools and wider social networks.   (ibid.: 15)

These findings confirm the work of Burns (1982) which demonstrated that pupils who have taken part in programmes to raise their awareness of emotions and to enhance their self-esteem quite simply achieve higher scores on standardised achievement tests.

The more pupils understand their emotions, the less likely they are to feel disaffected from the learning process. Instead of channelling their emotional difficulties into bullying, conflict and confrontation with school authorities, they will be able to find ways of engaging in a positive way with the opportunities for many different forms of learning being provided within the school.

The circle helps everyone to take part. In my old school when we did PSE, we used to sit in rows in desks. In the circle we can see everybody and it is much easier to talk.

(Sakira, 12 years)

I think that when you learn things this way it stays in your mind, like how to clean your teeth properly.

(Sally, 12 years)

The power of Circle Time to promote personal and social development

The circle process is a good way of promoting dialogue between the subgroups that we have already noted form within a class of young people, helping to break down some of the entrenched ways of relating. Once ground rules are established for respectful listening, and there are no 'put-downs', they relax and begin to tolerate each person's individuality. This then allows them to value the distinctive contributions, which others who are different from them can make. They learn the skills of empathy. Increased empathy increases tolerance of difference whether social, cultural or racial. If I understand someone else's world, I don't need to crush it. This has enormous potential to help create a society that celebrates its diversity.

I liked passing the egg around and voicing our opinions. I thought it was cool how people had different opinions about different things.

(Sarah, 12 years)

The games and strategies of Circle Time mix up the friendship groups in a very fluid, non-confrontational way. The issues and problems that are highlighted in circle sessions emerge from the pupils themselves. They therefore become the most important focus. The framework of sitting within a circle, taking a turn to speak and joining in all the activities convey important messages regarding authority and control to all the participants. The teacher's role is facilitative, encouraging pupils to feel that they too, have the authority and self-control to attempt to solve the behaviour, learning and relationship problems that concern them. By contributing to this problem-solving process, individuals are motivated to take more self and collective responsibility.

It was instantly obvious that both their concentration and honesty improved dramatically as soon as their social group was divided. They seem to interact with people who aren't their friends much better as a result of Circle Time. It has helped tremendously with the less confident members of the tutor group and it is a much more interesting way for the teacher to deliver the content of the curriculum. I don't honestly know yet, whether I can claim it is raising self-esteem, but at least they'd rather stay in the circle than go anywhere else and it gives me the opportunity to know their strengths and weaknesses much better than I would with work sheets and course books.   (Dominic Salles, year 8 tutor)

The debate over pupils' ability to regulate their own behaviour has long continued. The question asked is whether people are free agents, with self-determined behaviour, or whether forces outside themselves control them. Research cited in Lefcourt (1982) indicates that people's reactions and responses to situations is affected by their perceived control and perceived ability to cope.

Some people see their behaviour and environment as under external control e.g. by luck, chance, unknown but powerful others etc. Others believe they have internal control via skill, ability, experience and inherent potential to control behaviour and influence events.

Rotter (1966) used the term 'locus of control' to describe individuals' assessments of the power they can exert over their lives. Those with inner locus of control are less anxious about their ability to learn, are more confident in social and learning situations, have more self-control, are more likely to delay gratification, are more likely to ask questions of people, are better at retaining information and have superior academic achievement.

Those with external locus of control are inclined to say things like 'He made me do it', 'It wasn't my fault, she started it', 'I can't do it because I haven't got a ruler/pen etc.' These people have more difficulty with interpersonal relationships and learning situations. They tend to be less self-accepting than those with inner locus of control and more likely to give the 'Yes, but . . .' response to new ideas (Crandall *et al.* 1962, cited in Lefcourt 1982).

Most people are not, of course, at either one end of the spectrum or the other; rather they are inclined to interpret situations in one direction or the other. DeCharms (1972, cited in Hopson and Scally 1981) illustrated that teachers can teach children to take personal responsibility for their actions by enabling them to set realistic goals, discussing everyday events and encouraging them to use 'I' statements so that they own their feelings, actions and learning.

The circle encourages pupils to reflect on their behaviour, they offer and receive an array of advice and suggestions as to how they might change unsatisfactory behaviour. They identify personal targets for improvement and support each other in attempts to reach those targets. They recognise the achievements of their peers and praise them accordingly. There is a gradual shift of the onus of responsibility for discipline from the teacher to the young people themselves. They begin to learn and understand the consequences of their behaviour and take responsibility for themselves and others.

> This will help the student–teacher relationship become stronger and closer . . . this 30 minute period can have an effect on our entire lives.   (Nizia, 14 years)

Recognition from outside observers

The 1996 OFSTED Inspection Schedule as set out in the OFSTED Handbook made the importance of personal and social education and its contribution to pupils' personal and social development more explicit than previously. Schools are required to promote the personal and social development of their pupils. Inspections report on outcomes and those factors which contribute to the outcomes in terms of the quality of provision and management in schools. Aspects of the Quality Circle Time Model (outlined in Chapter 2) have been highlighted in OFSTED reports as a contributing factor in pupils' personal, moral and social development.

> **OFSTED Report: Rooks Heath High School, February 1999**
>
> Teachers are willing to adopt new methods, especially when pupils have benefited from them in middle schools. Recently, the personal, social education programme has been improved by the use of 'Circle Time', where pupils sit in a circle and follow formal rules for discussion. This is unusual in secondary schools and is a good example of teachers' willingness to maintain good practice started elsewhere. The pupils respond well, offering comments and displaying high levels of mutual trust and support. Social education is a strength of the school.'

Recent research indicates that successful schools are characterised by a healthy climate and a strong ethos, which respects and nurtures good relationships with clear, safe and secure boundaries. We cannot transmit moral codes through exhortation or cajole young people into becoming good citizens. Instead we need to provide them with a range of different opportunities to explore their feelings about how they live their lives and how they engage with other people. As a group process, Circle Time helps to generate a sense of 'belonging' which encourages individuals to become active members of the class and school community. This 'hands on' participation in democratic processes in the microcosm of the classroom or school helps to develop individual and corporate responsibility and hopefully, better citizens of the wider community.

> **OFSTED Report: Northgate Middle School**
>
> The school provides many opportunities for moral development. Issues are openly discussed as part of the curriculum and in Circle Times. Moral values are promoted by teachers through their relationships with pupils and during lessons. In discussions older pupils show good understanding of the issues facing individuals and discuss sensitively issues such as racism and bereavement.

> **OFSTED Report: Warren Comprehensive**
>
> The excellent quality of the relationships within the school is evidence that pupils feel respected and valued. This enables them to reflect positively on their experience of life. Circle Time, an exercise to raise self-esteem, is used by form tutors.

Does my school need to implement these ideas?

We live in an educational climate where social inclusion is high on the agenda. The debate includes issues such as school attendance, managing pupil behaviour, discipline and the use of exclusion. In the Green Paper *Excellence for All Children* (DfEE 1998), David Blunkett proposed shifting the focus in meeting special educational needs from procedures to practical support, and wherever possible from remediation to prevention and early intervention. The draft guidance on *Social*

9

Inclusion; Pupil Support (DfEE 1999) states, under classroom behaviour management, that 'Heads and governors will wish to consider whether adopting behaviour management techniques such as "The Whole School Quality Circle Time" model might help to improve and maintain high standards of behaviour and discipline.'

If you walk around a school while lessons are in progress, stand in corridors and listen at change of lesson time or visit the canteen during the lunch hour, it is easy to get an impression of the pervading ethos. It is a good idea to take stock of your school occasionally to assess how calm, respectful and productive the atmosphere is. One way of doing this is to go through the following list of indicators and see if they apply in your school.

Behaviour

- Are there queues of pupils outside the offices of senior staff, sent there by harassed teachers who have 'passed the problem on'?
- Does the school have a high incidence of bullying behaviour among pupils and/or adults?
- How do pupils relate to teaching and non-teaching staff?
- Are lessons spoilt by a high degree of low-level disruption?
- Is the main strategy to deal with pupils who are often in trouble during lessons to respond reactively by putting them in detention or issuing some other sanction?

PSHE

- Do pupils complain that PSHE lessons are boring and irrelevant?
- Do teachers always dictate the subject matter for PSHE lessons?
- Do staff avoid delivering PSHE whenever possible?
- Are staff late to tutorial lessons?
- Do staff rely heavily on work sheets for delivering PSHE?
- Do year 7 pupils find it difficult to settle into the school, to feel 'safe' and to make friends?

Support

- Is there a meeting for staff where they can discuss classroom or personal processes, rather then curriculum issues?
- Is there any system for early identification of pupils at risk of disaffection?
- Is there any system of early intervention for pupils who show signs of problem behaviour?
- Are pupils and their peers involved in devising strategies and/or setting realistic targets for behaviour?
- Is there a system for monitoring and rewarding the achievements of pupils who have behavioural or learning contracts?

The circle-time model addresses many of these issues by promoting self-discipline, more effective learning, team building and an ability to manage emotions, as explained in the following pages. Circle meetings provide a way of ensuring that all members of the school community are involved, listened to and motivated, thus helping to address some of the sense of isolation experienced by young people and staff.

2 | The wider vision: The Whole School Quality Circle Time Approach – an ecosystemic model

Up until now we have talked about 'the circle'. You probably have a picture in your mind of young people and adults sitting in circles interacting, relating and learning together. We would like to challenge you to expand this picture further by taking concepts embodied by the circle such as democracy, equality, respect, citizenship and apply them to all the systems in the school. We call this approach the Whole School Quality Circle Time Model and it is summarised at a glance in Figure 2.1. Each aspect of the model is unravelled one at a time in Chapters 3–10.

Why a 'whole-school approach'?

Research[1] has, time and again, indicated that effective schools are those that have created a positive atmosphere based on a sense of community and shared values. Proactive team building and a whole school commitment to promoting good behaviour was encouraged by the Elton Report (1989: 13), alongside 'personal and social education as a means of promoting the values of mutual respect, self-discipline and social responsibility which underlie good behaviour'.

The Quality Circle Time Model, Figure 2.1, represents a whole-school approach to positive behaviour and personal and social development. You will see from the diagram that the ideal school for us is one in which there is first a commitment to the self-esteem and morale of staff. It is vital that every child and adult has regular opportunities to speak and to be heard. Each should belong to a programme of timetabled circle-time meetings. Teachers have at least one staff meeting per half term where they don't have to discuss 'business' or curriculum issues, but can instead focus on their feelings. They talk through the various dilemmas, take time to understand certain difficult pupils and to ask for help with discipline or personal concerns without being judged or labelled as a 'failing teacher'. Some secondary schools may use year team meetings for this discussion, others departmental meetings, or house meetings. From the discussion comes a structured action plan that helps everyone to move forward.

The model involves not only teaching staff, but every adult that works in the school. Lunchtime supervisors, learning support assistants, office staff and site staff are all invited to circle meetings. Some schools negotiate a programme of meetings, which, even if they are only once or twice a half-term and half an hour at a time, can be very effective.

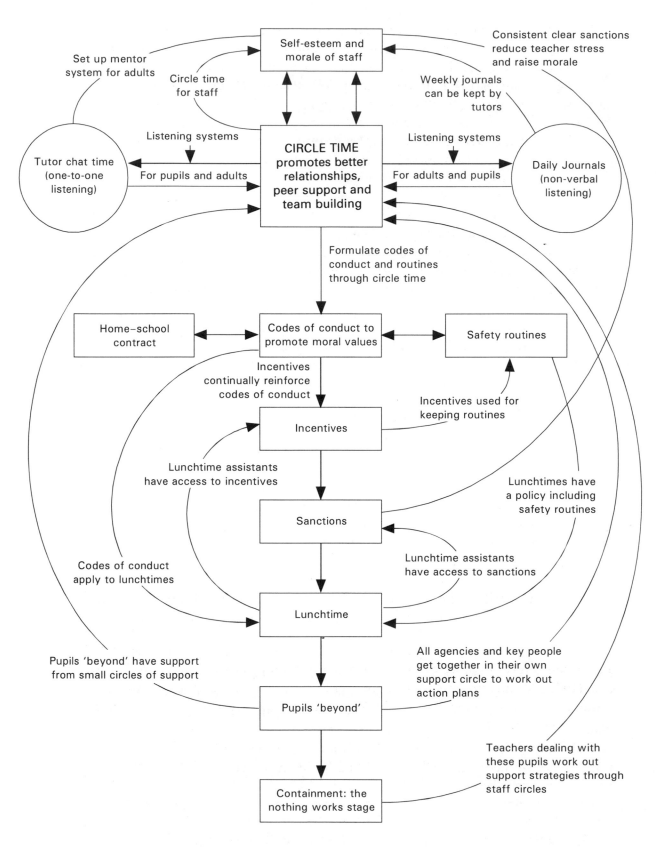

Figure 2.1 The Jenny Mosley Whole School Quality Circle Time Approach – an ecosystemic model

As staff and pupils become involved in their separate circle meetings, it is vital they link together by means of 'bridges'. The concept is that there should be a pivotal management circle, which receives the news, ideas and concerns for the other circles so that they can make informed management decisions based on a democratic consultation of all the members of the organisation. Therefore a person is selected from every circle to create a 'bridge' to the inner management circle by simply taking from their circle meeting, with the agreement of the other circle members, all the points of change or information that need to be noted by the pivotal circle. At some stage they have to return across the bridge with some feedback or response to the concerns or ideas. Schools that operate a school council have gone some way towards this model and a representative from the school council circle could take pupil issues to the inner management circle.

Alongside the group listening system or circle meetings, there are opportunities for one-to-one listening in the form of appraisal meetings, mentoring, personal development planning and tutor chat time plus non-verbal listening in the form of journals.

These listening systems can only be a safe place for meaningful discussion, however, if there is a measure of emotional 'safety' in the school. The school community needs to agree, make explicit and constantly reinforce a code of moral values and a set of procedural routines so that it can function with common aims. The moral values and procedures are then shared with parents in the home–school agreement so that there is a common understanding of school expectation. Once the codes of conduct are made explicit, they can be held in place and reinforced using systems of incentives and sanctions. Clearly communicated expectation and well-defined boundaries make it much easier for young people to develop acceptable standards of behaviour.

Why an ecosystemic approach?

We maintain that the Whole School Quality Circle Time Model represents an ecosystemic approach. As this concept is relatively new in education, we have at this point decided to explore the concept more fully.

The theoretical origins of applying a systemic approach to human behaviour rests in the work of Ludwig Von Bertalanffy (1950, 1968) and Gregory Bateson (1972, 1979) and in the clinical practice of pioneering family therapists such as Selvini-Palazzoli *et al.* (1973), Minuchin (1974) and De Shazer (1982, 1985). The application to a school context was developed in America by Molnar and Lindquist (1989) and in Britain by Cooper and Upton (1990, 1992, 1994).

Central to the concept of an ecosystemic approach to human behaviour is the premise that humans are essentially social beings. They are dependent on their social environment for their mental well-being in the same way as they depend on the physical environment for their physical survival. They are not wholly free to behave as they choose, but are constrained by, and have an influence on, the social network in which they operate. It is similar to the biological notion of an ecosystem where the life-cycles of plants, animals and other organisms are linked to each other and to the non-living constituents of the environment to form a set of natural systems which interrelate. A change in any one part of a system has a 'knock-on' effect throughout the whole system and may lead to reverberations in allied systems.

The two essential human needs, first for a recognised personal identity and secondly for a sense of belonging to a social group, cause people to operate largely in a group context or 'system'. Individuals depend on the group to supply particular needs i.e. recognition of their individuality and the sense of belonging, so the group becomes the central focus of activity. The foundational social unit in secondary school is the tutorial group. An ecosystemic approach offers new ways of thinking about the interactional processes in a tutor group which has the potential to promote, sustain or redefine the behaviour of individuals.

Historically, there has been a tendency in the teaching profession to see some pupils as 'having' behaviour problems. If the cause of the problem behaviour is perceived to reside in the pupil, the 'cure' will be in dealing with the individual and the school need not question its structures, relationships and systems. Systemic approaches see behaviour as a product of interaction. Consequently if teachers wish to change the behaviour of pupils, they need to consider whether the behaviour is in any way a product of the environment which exists in the classroom, the school, or in the teacher– pupil interaction (Hanko 1985). This view produces a shift towards collaborative approaches to problem-solving. Pupil behaviour, which is defined as problematic, is always goal directed. This means that from the pupil's viewpoint it is understandable, rational and, above all, necessary. What appears problematic for the teacher may well be a solution to the pupil or for a subsystem in the classroom or the school. In a systemic approach it becomes important then to hear how each individual perceives a situation in order to understand the interactions and explore alternative, more effective means of achieving the goals which the behaviour is perceived to serve. The circle meeting in this model provides a place for listening to individual perceptions and exploring alternative solutions. It permits pupils and teachers to view one another differently and so to reframe both 'problems' and 'solutions' while providing an image of the individual as a worthy and valuable human being.

This way of thinking has real implications, not only for the tutor group, but for the whole school, where all the systems can be seen to be interconnected and to interrelate. Changes in one system create intended and unintended outcomes in other parts of the institution. For instance, creating Circle Time as a respectful forum for listening might well generate difficulties in the sanction system because young people now question whether it is fair. Similarly implementing ground rules for good communication in PSHE may well generate hot debate about the way pupils are spoken to in other lessons. The positive side of the ecosystemic coin is that change in one system will have impact in many other areas and possibly eventually all areas of school life. If the first change generates more respect, higher self-esteem and greater motivation, there is the possibility of examining all the systems in the same light of respect and thus generating a more positive working community over a period of time.

Molnar and Lindquist (1989) put it succinctly when they suggest 'when you want something to change, you must change something'. Changing one part of the system alters the interactional meaning with repercussions throughout the whole.

When considering policy that affects personal social education, it is important to involve all members of the school community and every part of the school day. The ideal would be to implement the model throughout the school as whole-school policy. We are realistic enough, however, to know that the ideal rarely exists, so where tutors and teachers are unable to influence school policy, many of the strategies can be employed on a classroom basis. As we unravel the model a section at a time in Chapters 3–10, the reader is encouraged to think of individual applications that would affect his/her personal or professional practice and to look at the wider context of the whole school.

Notes

1. Dawson, N. and McNess, E. (1998) *A Report on the Use of Circle Time in Wiltshire Primary Schools*. The Scottish Office, unpublished research. University of Bristol, Graduate School of Education, CLIO.

3 Unravelling the Model: Raising self-esteem and morale of staff

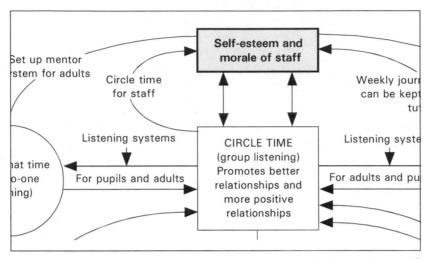

See Figure 2.1, page 12

High self-esteem staff encourage high self-esteem pupils

> The teacher–pupil encounter is permeated on the teacher's side by his general outlook and philosophy of life . . . Teachers possess self-concepts which affect their own and the pupils' behaviour, their ability to build sound relationships with the pupils, their style of teaching, and their perceptions and expectations of themselves as teachers and of children as learners.
>
> (Burns 1982)

> Research tells us that positive self-concepts in teachers helps not only their own classroom performance as a confident, unanxious, respected guide to learning, but also pupil performance which flourishes in all respects when the pupil has someone who projects trust and belief in their capacity and has a warm, supportive ethos to enhance his view of himself as someone of worth. Expectancies from such teachers lead to high pupil self-esteem and performance.
>
> (ibid.: 254)

It is all very well having good ideas about whole-school approaches and reforming the relationships and behaviour management in secondary schools, but it cannot happen if the adults working in the school have no energy or motivation to bring it about. It is impossible to expect adults to respond positively, warmly and calmly to pupils if they themselves are emotionally and physically exhausted and/or lacking in support. This applies to all the adults, not just the teaching staff. The Whole School Quality Circle Time Model outlined in Chapter 2 therefore first focuses on the mental health of all the adults in the school.

How can you gauge the self-esteem of adults?

Sound self-esteem

Good self-esteem brings a sense of competence and worth. An individual with good self-esteem views his/herself as a capable, likeable and worthwhile person. These people will welcome and enjoy new experiences and be able to relate well to others. They exude confidence and optimism, which brings a positive approach to personal and professional life. Moreover, people with good self-esteem are able to learn from criticism, mistakes and failures and to view them in a calm and realistic way. They hold the different aspects of life in perspective and so maintain a sense of balance. Some of the indicators of high self-esteem would include the following behaviours:

- **people who have confidence to cope with problems and surmount difficulties;**
- **people who can cope with getting it wrong without becoming defensive;**
- **people who can change what they think, even strongly held values, in the light of new information or experience;**
- **people who do not 'agonise' over the past or the future, they can 'go with the flow';**
- **people who think of themselves as valuable and of equal worth even when they are not good at a particular task or skill;**
- **people who notice and respond to the needs of others.**

Poor self-esteem

Poor self-esteem brings a sense of uselessness and incompetence. People with low self-esteem can exhibit a variety of behaviours. They can lack confidence which results in nagging self-doubt, suffer from occasional self-pity and have difficulty in sustaining meaningful relationships with others. On the other hand, they can be loud, opinionated and bossy, covering up their sense of inadequacy with dominating behaviour. Such people often protect themselves from hurt by being aggressive and 'putting other people down', or withdrawing into a lonely 'shell'. Secretly they regard themselves as a failure or as totally misunderstood and think everyone else is more successful than they are. This negative thinking results in a pattern of behaviour which becomes a self-fulfilling prophecy and ensures that they continue to fail.

Some of the following pointers are indicative of low self-esteem, though there are many others:

- **people who rarely admit they are wrong;**
- **people who see difficulties or obstacles as catastrophes;**
- **people who are hypercritical of others;**
- **people who defend their shaky self-image by pointing out other people's faults when they are challenged about their own;**
- **people who take things very personally;**
- **people who refuse to acknowledge any failure and weakness in themselves;**
- **people who 'feed on' flattery and seem to need adulation;**
- **people who are wary of putting themselves forward or volunteering despite being competent to do the task.**

Undoubtedly there are teachers and those in management positions that recognise the importance of developing positive self-esteem in themselves and their colleagues as well as their students. Though such efforts are valuable and worthwhile, consider how much more impact could be made if every member of the school was committed to creating an environment where everyone was regularly listened to and encouraged, given respect and support.

Why is it particularly hard to have good self-esteem in teaching?

One of the questions we ask teachers in our training programme is why they entered the profession. Their responses often reveal a vision which was once infused with

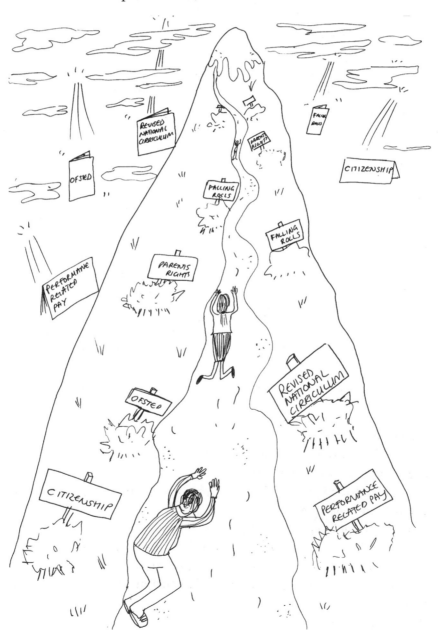

their own pleasure in learning; a regard for children; and a belief that they could effect positive changes. Now we see teachers metaphorically wearily trudging up a huge mountain, so bowed down by pressures and worries that they are unable to glimpse the vision they are supposed to be trying to reach. Snowstorms of paper whistle around and obscure their view. Boulders come out of the cloud that obscures the top of the mountain and whiz past their heads. These boulders take the form of large ring-binder files containing new National Curriculum syllabi, pupils with severe emotional and behavioural problems, Local Education Authority (LEA) policies on inclusion, negative media coverage, targets for pupils performance, and inequality of resources. Every time the teacher begins to make some headway up the mountain, s/he become snarled up in a prickly bush behind which lurks a parent claiming certain rights, OFSTED inspectors brandishing sheaves of paper and transfer pupils who have been excluded from a nearby school.

It is not surprising then that some hard-pressed teachers find themselves resorting to defensive actions in an effort to survive the rigours of the classroom. Yet, the more we become caught in negative interactions, the more our self-esteem is lowered.

It is important to 'take stock' of your own self-esteem so that you can assess the sort of support, help or action plan you may need.

So how can we look after ourselves?

If you can view yourself as a much-needed resource for pupils and other adults, then you will understand that you can't keep on giving out. Like any resource, you need replenishing from time to time. Energy is one of the most important resources you have and in order to sustain the energy you require you must learn how to revitalise yourself.

Golden moments or 'time out'

Develop a calming ritual at key times in the day and use these times to switch off from work-related problems and the nagging voices in your head. Calming rituals can be anything that might relax you – for example a cup of coffee and the crossword, a long shower or listening to your favourite music tape. Some teachers like to arrive early so that they can set up the classroom, then have a calm cup of coffee before the pupils arrive. At the end of the day it is also useful to develop a ritual that marks the end of school so that you go home in a positive frame of mind.

Case study

One head teacher we know drives home and as he passes a particular spot, he imagines taking his work out of the car and placing it in a burrow, out of sight at the side of the road. He the proceeds home as a 'home person'. This does not mean that he never takes work home, but he does as much as he can while in school and once home, the focus of his attention is family. In the morning, as he passes the same spot, he visualises picking up the work again, putting it back in the car and driving to school as a 'work person'.

Golden moments are based on the idea of concentrating on each of your senses, bringing them alive, while entering one moment of pleasure. For example, take a hot drink outside; concentrate on the taste of the drink, the heat of the cup, the touch of the breeze, the scent of plants, the sounds of the birds/traffic and the sight of the clouds and sky. By concentrating on your senses and talking yourself through them, it is possible to shut out negative thoughts associated with problems. It is disconcerting to meet teachers on courses who say they cannot find one Golden Moment in a day. Maintaining our mental health demands that we do create these moments for ourselves.

Breathing techniques

Another useful and quick way of ridding the body of tension is to learn deep breathing techniques and to use them while concentrating on relaxing your body. Sit on a chair, evenly distributing your weight and slowly breathe in to the count of 3 or 4, keeping your mouth closed. Imagine the oxygen going through all the pathways in your body making you feel lighter and more energetic. Then slowly expel the air through your mouth – again to the same count. It is helpful if you can learn to use breathing and relaxation techniques when standing so that the adrenaline flood that comes under stress and triggers the flight or fight response is brought under control. Once the adrenaline abates in your system, the blood flows once again to the thinking centres of the brain and rational decisions can be made!

Keeping clear boundaries

The most important survival technique is to organise your time effectively. As we travel around the country, we meet dedicated teachers who work all day at school, take marking and preparation and reports home, work all evening and even work much of the weekend. The difficulty is that teaching is a never ending job so unless

you decide how much time you will allocate to extra-curricular school-related work and stick to it, you run the risk of 'burn-out' and stress-related illness. Prioritise what needs to be done, so that you deal with important and urgent items first, and be strict with yourself about leaving tasks which are not vital for another day. One pitfall to avoid is the bag or box that pulsates guilt. Every school has at least one 'bags person' and we are all tempted to become one. The big box or several bags are full of things to do, which we lug from classroom to sitting room and back again. It is so daunting a burden that we can't face tackling it. It merely sits in the corner of our vision distracting us from getting any real pleasure from our leisure time, as every time we catch sight of it we feel guilty. The trick is to prioritise. Only tackle what is undeniably necessary, those things that failure to do would be observable to all. Many of the things in the box are good intentions; they are not strictly needed, so throw them out!

4 Setting up the listening systems

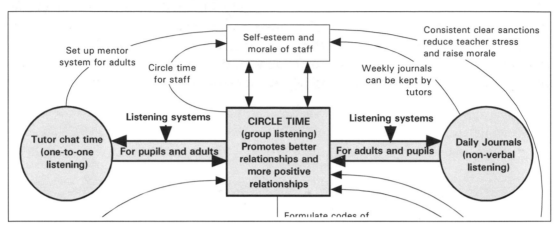

See Figure 2.1, page 12

Listening systems – an overview

If we accept that being listened to is the key to feeling valued and worthwhile, then we encounter a problem. Frazzled, exhausted teachers will find it difficult to listen well and in order to ensure good listening it cannot be left to chance and the fluctuating levels of teacher energy. If we are honest, we know that as teachers, we often appear harassed, busy and unapproachable to the eyes of pupils. Young people are put off trying to speak to us and the ensuing sense of frustration or even isolation can drive them to demand the much needed attention by anti-social means such as sulking, defying or arguing. After all, negative attention is better than no attention. Perhaps the greatest challenge at this stage of the model is to ask yourself 'Can I, as a teacher, role model good listening? Am I respectful enough to set up listening systems?' (Appendix A provides a helpful checklist for evaluating your ability to be a good listening role-model).

Three listening systems are suggested in the whole school model (Chapter 2):

- **Circle Time – the group listening system;**
- **one-to-one tutor time – for private conversations;**
- **daily journals – for non-verbal listening.**

The school can also implement a whole-school listening system in the form of a school council with elected members from each tutor group. In order for school councils to be effective, they must have status and power. If it is a 'cosmetic' gesture, pupils will soon lose confidence and interest in it. The acid test of how much power a school council has is whether pupils want to represent their form or be represented on it.

So how do we make listening systems work?

Circle Time – a group listening system

The detail of how to establish and run Circle Time in the secondary school is given in Part II of this book: The Practice. There you will find many ideas for games, scripts and activities. Here it is enough to point out that the circle meeting has structures and strategies that encourage the development of positive relationships, self-discipline, self-regulating behaviour, conflict resolution, assertive communication and democratic group process alongside the skills of speaking, listening, observing, thinking and concentrating. The meeting takes place usually once a week to consider issues relating to personal, social and moral education and matters of whole-school concern.

- **It involves the whole class, including the teacher, meeting in an inward-facing circle so that each group member can see the faces of every speaker.**
- **The act of physically sitting in a circle emphasises equality and collective responsibility. As one student said, 'There is no head to a circle.'**
- **Pupils have the opportunity to speak and a commitment to listen to each other's views.**
- **The teacher is required to adopt a facilitative style rather than a didactic approach. This is one occasion when the teacher's opinions and solutions to problems are equal to anyone else's.**
- **It involves the whole class and adults agreeing to a 'contract' of ground rules which facilitate open discussion.**
- **Honesty, cooperation and trust are encouraged in an emotionally 'safe' environment where feelings can be explored and risks taken.**
- **In Circle Time, the teacher's ability to give pupils warmth, respect and positive regard is all important in building pupil self-esteem and encouraging changes in thinking and behaving.**

Two streams of issues emerge from the circle meeting. One is to do with personal matters relevant to the pupils in the group. Individuals or the whole group may set targets or action plans which would be followed up at subsequent circle meetings. The second stream is to do with management issues in the school. They might relate to overcrowding in certain areas of the building, bullying, queuing systems or safety in corridors and on stairs between lessons. These would need to be taken to the school council or communicated to the relevant member of the senior management team so that the listening system produces some action or feedback.

One-to-one listening

One of the main ground rules adopted in Circle Time is that no names may be used with a negative connotation. This is not a shaming, blaming and defaming forum! However this rule automatically denies pupils the right to tell you about any important personal concerns they may have. Circle Time therefore needs to be backed up by private one-to-one listening or 'chat' time. This is not easy to organise but some teachers have tried various ways of making themselves available.

Case studies

- One tutor agreed with her tutor group to take her coffee to the tutor room one break-time a week. She was always available no matter whether pupils came to talk to her or not. At first there was little response, but over a period of time, pupils took advantage of the opportunity to speak privately. The teacher found that the key to success was to make sure that the visit was not associated with 'problems' or 'telling on people'. She was available to talk about any issues: homework or curriculum related; whole-school management; personal good news; personal difficulties; or private information.

- **A rota system** Another group of tutors agreed to provide one-to-one listening for a whole year group. The five members of the tutor team talked with their tutor groups and agreed to take a break time each in a week. When it was their turn to be on 'listening duty', they took their coffee and spent the break in the designated room so that they were available to anyone in the year group who wanted to talk privately.

- Some schools put one-to-one informal tutor listening alongside a more formalised Personal Development Plan interview that takes place once or twice each year to monitor pupil's progress and personal development.

- Other schools have developed peer listening systems. They have trained volunteers from the older year groups in listening skills and set up a 'drop in' listening room manned by year 11 or by sixth-form students where they are available in the school. The school then provided clear guidelines and regular supervision for these older pupils.

We are not suggesting that teachers should be social workers or psychotherapists. However, the whole notion of setting up listening systems, particularly one-to-one listening presupposes that teachers have the skills to be good listeners. Effective schools seem to be able to combine high expectations with a sympathetic atmosphere and there is a need to strike this balance. The Elton Report (1989) noted this need and made the following recommendation regarding listening:

> We are convinced that there are skills, which all teachers need, involved in listening to young people and encouraging them to talk about their hopes and concerns before coming to a judgement about their behaviour. We consider that these basic counselling skills are particularly valuable for creating a supportive school atmosphere. The skills needed to work effectively with adults, whether teachers or parents, are equally crucial. We therefore recommend that initial teacher training establishments should introduce all their students to basic counselling skills and their value. We regard such skills as particularly important for all senior pastoral staff (deputy heads, heads of houses and year).

Non-verbal listening

Often pupils prefer to write than to talk. Many schools operate a regular journal system where each pupil has a personal journal. The journals are kept in a designated but accessible safe place so that they cannot be read by anyone else. The pupils can write to the tutor at any time to record an achievement, ask a question or write a message. The journal is then put in an agreed place. Having read the message, the teacher can either respond with a written reply or arrange a private chat with the pupil.

Extracts from daily journals from pupils in Year 7

Dear Mrs ...
        I am thick. Now I am writing this, I'm going to admit it, I am thick. I don't like saying it but I have to face up to it soon won't I? And what about when I take my exams? I won't be able to do them will I? I feel like crying sometimes when I can't get my maths right. But I do like this school.

I think you've forgotten some of the really good things you can do. Would you like a chat?

It has been O.K. today. we have been last into dinner all week. It's not fun. It's nearly as bad as standing outside of Mr W's office. That's dead boring.

I'm glad it's o.K. today. If you think the dinner queuing system is not fair, why don't you bring it up with the school council rep?

---

5 Establishing codes of conduct

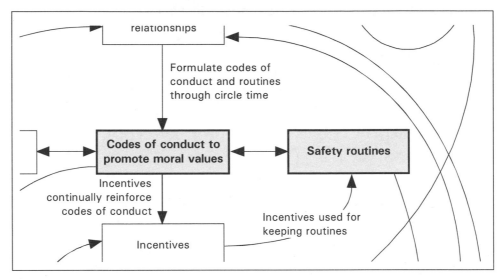

relationships

Formulate codes of
conduct and routines
through circle time

**Codes of conduct to
promote moral values**

Safety routines

Incentives
continually reinforce
codes of conduct

Incentives used for
keeping routines

Incentives

See Figure 2.1, page 12

Rules, Rules, Rules

Whenever we have used part of Circle Time to listen to young people's views about school rules and routines, we invariably encounter confusion. Despite schools' best intentions and lists of rules in the front of academic year planners or homework diaries etc., pupils rarely seem clear about their school's expectations. It is also interesting to note that wherever we go in secondary schools, we find disagreement over rules among the staff.

Perhaps the confusion and dissent becomes less surprising when you examine the list of rules in a behaviour policy that young people are expected to remember! In order to make it easier to agree, disseminate and commonly own a set of rules, one unique recommendation of our model is to separate the debate into two parts. One side of the argument concerns the set of rules that cover practical safety. These rules, routines or procedures enable the school community to function in an orderly and safe way. The other side of the debate refers to a set of rules we will call the codes of conduct. These are the moral values that inform and develop the 'culture' of a classroom or school.

More often than not, school rules are a mixture of moral values and institutional routines. Both are extremely important for the smooth running of the school and the safety of the people who work there. Both sets of rules also inform behaviour, yet they are different.

One of the major differences between these two sets of rules is to do with the place of negotiation. Moral values are the moral absolutes of the institution. They are not negotiable. They underpin the ethos of the school, apply in all parts of the school buildings and grounds and reflect the law of the wider community. On the other

26

hand, routines need to be negotiated. They will be different in different parts of the school and will vary from teacher to teacher.

So how do we make it work?

Moral values

'Moral' describes the principles which inform judgements about what is good or bad. People's attitudes, are largely built on what they value. These values and attitudes also inform a pupil's behaviour, they describe what we would like pupil's to *be* in their adult life. We expect pupils to work hard, to behave appropriately towards peers and adults, to look after property and to develop an acceptable set of personal values.

Many secondary school teachers argue that making codes of conduct explicit is unnecessary: 'Pupils should know how to behave by secondary age.' There is a problem with this premise, however, because secondary schools receive pupils from a large number of primary feeder schools, each operating a different behaviour policy. There is also often a conflict between the values and expectations of the home and the school. So, whatever we think secondary pupils 'should know', it seems unfair to run a school without making expectation clear. For that matter, no system of rewards or sanctions is meaningful or respectful without an agreed set of values, which everyone in the community works towards.

This model proposes that schools agree a set of values which everyone in the school upholds. This would include office staff, support staff, ancillary staff, site staff and teaching staff. Some schools approach values through the notion of rights and responsibilities. Others emphasise that certain behaviours are prohibited by the law of the land. The school prepares young people for their place as adult citizens by adopting a similar set of moral 'laws'. Other schools prefer to have values that are explicitly stated, displayed in every area of the school and taught through the PSHE or pastoral programme.

Whatever the philosophy, Circle Time in year 7 is the ideal forum for introducing the school's codes of conduct. Schools at the 'cutting edge' of developing the circle-time model spend time in the Christmas term of year 7 exploring the concept of rules and why they are necessary in a school. They then move on to specific codes of conduct, which are learned and reinforced through activities and games. Schools devise their own wording for their codes of conduct, but they embody common values that all secondary schools would promote. They reflect the values that underpin a democratic society and cover:

- **respect for self;**
- **respect for others;**
- **respect for work;**
- **respect for property.**

Schools may wish, as primary schools do, to set them out as 'Golden Rules' with a positive balanced by a negative.

For example:

- **do listen; don't interrupt; or**
- **do work hard; don't waste yours or other people's time.**

In special schools, pictures and photographs of pupils demonstrating examples of good behaviour are used to illustrate the rules. Whichever way the codes of conduct are displayed, a copy needs to go home in the home–school agreement so that parents are also in no doubt as to the moral expectations of the school.

Routines

The routines describe what we want pupils to *do* in different parts of the school. They are not the same in all areas, so the routines of the science laboratory will be different from the routines of the school canteen and different again from the drama studio. Secondary schools make these routines very clear and they are explicitly stated, often posted on the wall of the area concerned. This is because the routines describe the behaviour which will keep pupils safe when using the space or equipment in this area of the school. Since any one member of staff works in a prescribed area according to his/her subject specialism, there is often no need for any whole-school agreement about routines. Some might apply throughout the school such as walking in corridors, wearing uniform correctly, not chewing gum or not interfering with health and safety equipment such as fire extinguishers. Many however, are agreed within a faculty area and do not concern another faculty such as the specific routines associated with using gym apparatus or procedures in the different technology rooms.

The routines can be agreed within a faculty or in consultation with pupils and then written in the front of the exercise book at the beginning of the year.

6 Creating and implementing incentives

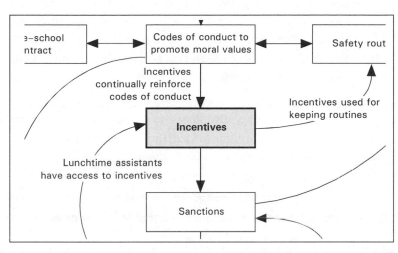

See Figure 2.1, page 12

What's the point of incentives?

Incentives or rewards are the good news that we give to pupils, their peers and their parents about pupils' personal, social and academic development. The rewards accompany the positive side of the codes of conduct or rules. While secondary schools might find the notion of 'Golden Rules' too simplistic, it is worth remembering that many pupils have not arrived at a stage of moral development where they have internalised the moral values required by society and promoted in schools. Often, as we have already noted, a set of different values from those of the school is practised within the pupil's background. When the rules are stated as a list of behaviours such as 'Don't smoke on the school premises or on the buses or outside the school in the immediate vicinity', it tends to become a challenge to see if I can do it and not get caught!

There is a problem, however. As soon as incentives are mentioned, it becomes clear that secondary colleagues cannot agree the 'currency' of a house point. What constitutes achievement good enough to receive a reward? Consequently some members of staff give many merits/house points and some give virtually none. Such a system becomes very unfair in the eyes of the pupil. If you are a 'perfect' pupil, one of those fortunate souls who happens to fit the system as hand fits glove and are neat, organised and well presented into the bargain, you will receive rewards. On the other hand, if you are completely disorganised, untidy and difficult to motivate, everyone is falling over themselves to reward the tiniest hint of progress. The 'middle-plodder' pupil can be forgiven for finding this a very unjust system! Perhaps the most difficult task facing the secondary teacher is to ensure that these 'middle-plodder' pupils receive regular good news about their work and behaviour. They are so easily overlooked that they can go through the entire five years of Key Stages 3 and 4 feeling that they are invisible!

Rewarding the 'middle-plodder' pupil

One school decided to take this whole issue of noticing and rewarding the 'middle plodder' pupil very seriously. They devised the following chart. The class sheet (Figure 6.1) is taken from one lesson to the next by selected pupils. It is placed on the teacher's desk and s/he notes any outstanding behaviour in the 'excellent' column and any unacceptable behaviour in the 'disappointing' column. The rest are automatically good. In reality, this is very little effort since the majority of pupils are 'good' i.e. they arrive on time, remain mostly on task without interfering with or disrupting anyone else's learning, and have done their homework.

Names	Excellent	Good	Disappointing
Mark Adams	✓		
Shakira Begum			
Shane Carter			✓ calling out

Figure 6.1   An idea for acknowledging good behaviour and diligent work.

The list goes to the form tutor at the end of each day and pupils who have not received any 'disappointing' or 'excellent' comments (i.e. the 'good' column is unticked) are automatically rewarded with one merit or house point. The 'excellent' are given two house points and these add up to a graded certificate or privilege at the end of each half term. The 'disappointing' are highlighted for some kind of sanction.

This system works particularly well in year 7 when pupils are generally taught in tutor groups. It becomes slightly more difficult to administer in higher years when a teaching set may be made up of pupils from several different tutor groups.

So how can we make incentives work?

Initially the incentives can take the form of tangible rewards. These help to spread the good news about the pupil to other pupils and to staff, especially if they are given publicly such as in assemblies. As the pupil becomes older, they are much less keen on being given public acclaim and the rewards become more intrinsic.

The following principles are some that we have found to be useful in planning an incentive system.

- **The pupils know best what motivates them so carry out a survey among the pupils to find out the best incentives for your school.**
- **Be aware that the incentives that work well with Key Stage 3 are different from those that motivate Key Stage 4 pupils, so make sure both groups are surveyed.**
- **Incentives need to reward the quiet, hardworking, 'middle-plodder' pupils who neither exhibit academic excellence nor disruptive behaviour and are therefore often overlooked.**
- **Every pupil is entitled to some good news about him/herself. On courses staff some-times say there is 'nothing "good" about some pupils, so I can't give them rewards'. It**

is tempting to ask 'What makes a person valuable?' 'Are the targets you set too high?' Good teaching is surely about creating small achievable targets then noticing the pupil's success. If a teacher cannot find good news to give back to a pupil, it tells us more about the unrealistic expectations of that teacher than about the progress of the pupil. 'Encouragers' are small rewards which are given quite frequently, such as house points or merits, for abiding by the codes of conduct of the school.

The following research on rewards and sanctions was completed by John of Gaunt School, Head of Year. Many thanks for giving permission to reproduce it.

Rewards and sanctions

Our emotions are influenced by the rewards and sanctions we receive. Read the following list of preferred rewards of pupils in years 7–9, then answer the questions below.

- Letter of praise to parents
- Rewarded by a commendation
- Praised by Head of Year
- Name appearing on a notice board
- Mentioned in assembly
- Praised by subject teacher

- Having work on display
- Praised by form tutor
- Praised by other pupils
- Whole class praised
- Non-verbal praise, like a smile

Questions

1. Number the above points in your order of preference.
2. Write out the reward you preferred most, and say why you chose it.

_____

_____

Now read the list of sanctions disliked by year 7 and year 9 pupils, then answer the questions listed below.

- Removed from group
- Put on report – parents informed
- Given unpleasant jobs to do
- Told off in front of class/assembly
- After school detention
- Being kept in at lunchtime

- Sent to Year Head/Deputy Head
- Removal of privilege
- Given lines
- Told off privately
- Sent out of class
- Being moved to another set

Questions

1. Number the above points in the order you dislike them most.
2. Write out the sanction you dislike most and say why this is so.

_____

_____

Figure 6.2 Survey on rewards and sanctions, John of Gaunt School, Wiltshire.

Table 6.1 Survey of preferred incentives at John of Gaunt School, Wiltshire

Tutor Groups	T	H	J	N	G	S	Sub-total
Boys							
Letter of praise to parents	79	109	110	128	72	126	624 (1)
Reward by commendation	48	80	59	83	32	85	387 (4)
Praised by Year Head	63	101	102	91	74	107	538 (2)
Name on notice board	40	54	40	45	21	66	266 (7)
Mentioned in assembly	37	43	77	56	62	86	361 (6)
Praised by subject staff	51	81	68	78	47	81	406 (3)
Having work on display	33	25	30	53	34	58	233 (9)
Praised by Tutor	45	68	71	65	53	81	383 (5)
Praised by other pupils	28	58	43	31	27	58	245 (8)
Whole class praised	30	44	36	52	28	40	230 (10)
Non-verbal praise, e.g. smile	18	31	4	11	18	35	117 (11)
Girls							
Letter of praise to parents	141	114	92	45	83	99	574 (1)
Reward by commendation	90	94	66	50	28	56	384 (4)
Praised by Year Head	97	86	78	33	82	92	468 (2)
Name on notice board	66	54	40	34	41	28	263 (7)
Mentioned in assembly	70	54	69	28	38	26	285 (6)
Praised by subject staff	58	68	70	21	55	61	333 (5)
Having work on display	74	35	34	31	32	27	232 (8)
Praised by Tutor	78	72	68	45	65	68	436 (3)
Praised by other pupils	24	33	47	14	43	52	212 (9)
Whole class praised	38	36	33	35	16	30	188 (10)
Non-verbal praise, e.g. smile	36	18	30	21	11	20	136 (11)

'Specials' are rewards that are given less frequently such as certificates, positions of responsibility, letters of commendation etc. They can be given for an accumulation of 'encouragers' or for special events.

- **When adolescents are reluctant to receive incentives publicly, research has nevertheless shown that they like to have good news sent home to their parents where it has good repercussions and they are rewarded all over again.**
- **One of the most potent influences in the life of adolescents is the peer group. Circle Time encourages a culture of positive feedback from peers. Sometimes a tutor group will make 'Class Team Certificates', which are signed by members of the tutor group and presented within the group or at year assembly.**
- **Encourage pupils to value their own opinion of themselves as much as they value others' by providing opportunities to reflect and comment on their own performance.**

7 Creating and implementing sanctions

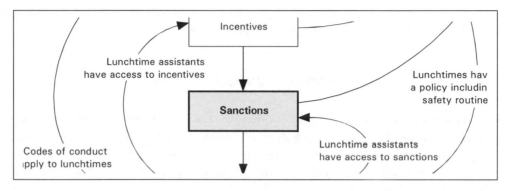

See Figure 2.1, page 12

Clearly negotiated and communicated sanctions are an essential requisite of positive school and classroom management. Perhaps here is a good place, however, to draw attention to some of the worrying aspects of current 'punishment' practices. If we try to diminish a behaviour by mild punishment and it does not prove effective, the logical step is to try more severe punishment. In other words, one is led into an ineffective escalation of punishments rather like the postcard notice 'Beatings will continue until morale improves' and as Watkins (1997) concludes 'punishment leads some people to believe there are only two possible responses in our repertoire: punitive action or inaction'. This is very disempowering.

If classroom control is focused on punishments it demands a high degree of 'policing' and teachers turn into monitors rather than managers of learning. Research has demonstrated that strongly authoritative or disciplinarian teachers create an atmosphere that is counter-productive to learning. Similarly for pupils, a focus on punishment may serve to generate compliance rather than self-regulated behaviour. So the challenge is to develop an ethos where disruption is less likely to happen and to put the choice of appropriate or inappropriate behaviour in the hands of the pupil.

If codes of conduct are made explicit and displayed, then broken by pupils without any consequences, the message is that rules are useless. Some pupils live chaotic lives without boundaries. Sanctions offer clear boundaries and a safe framework. Teenagers test their power and they have learned that if they nag for long enough, parents will give in. They need to know that school boundaries are secure, especially as for some young people, the only place they feel 'safe' is at school. Sanctions can allow a pupil to work off a 'debt', which can then be forgotten about; the 'slate' is wiped clean.

Sanctions also help to create safer teachers. By this we mean that if a teacher does not have a declared set of sanctions, pupils are never quite sure what sanction he/she will use. This leaves the system vulnerable to a teacher's inconsistency, which can be influenced by events and personal moods. The teacher is vulnerable to resorting to frequent, loud verbal 'tellings off'. This public spectacle can result in humiliation and angry resentment, which may later produce retaliatory behaviour.

Perhaps one of the most relevant questions is 'Are the sanctions really deterrents to undesirable behaviour, or have they become rewards?' In one school we visited, during a Circle Time discussion about sanctions, pupils were asked what happened if they misbehaved. They said that they were put out into the corridor. When asked if they minded this punishment they replied 'Course not, it is quiet in the corridor, you don't have to work and sometimes you meet your mate who's also been put out.' Clearly this sanction was not effective as a deterrent to poor behaviour!

How do I make sanctions work?

One of the most effective ways of checking that sanctions will work is to ask the pupils which ones they dislike the most. A survey among different year groups or key stages would reveal the most unpopular and arguably, the most effective sanction for the group. Table 7.1 shows the results of the piece of research into sanctions carried out in John of Gaunt School, Trowbridge using the survey sheet shown in Figure 6.2.

One of the recurrent problems teachers encounter when administering sanctions is the argument over what is and is not fair or whether the pupil was the only one doing it or the first! One way round this is to use a clear, irrefutable warning system so that the pupil is given the choice of changing his/her behaviour and so avoiding the sanction.

Table 7.1 Survey of sanctions at John of Gaunt School, Wiltshire

Tutor Groups	T	H	J	N	G	S	Sub-total
Boys							
Removed from group	73	71	57	44	50	90	375 (5)
Put on report – parents informed	62	89	111	53	79	93	487 (1)
Given unpleasant jobs to do	56	55	33	23	16	73	256 (6)
Told off in front of class	61	57	83	43	58	127	429 (4)
After school detention	57	88	94	56	54	103	452 (3)
Lunchtime detention	25	52	33	37	33	59	239 (7)
Sent to Head of Year or Department Head	57	79	71	64	69	122	462 (2)
Removal of privilege	35	30	30	33	24	42	194 (9)
Given lines	22	36	43	28	18	20	167 (11)
Told off privately	18	33	37	22	39	27	176 (10)
Sent out of class	25	48	43	27	23	39	205 (8)
Moved seats	4	43	12	19	11	14	103 (12)
Girls							
Removed from group	103	77	62	80	78	82	482 (2)
Put on report – parents informed	84	98	94	72	82	81	511 (1)
Given unpleasant jobs to do	40	24	23	35	25	19	166 (10)
Told off in front of class	96	97	90	63	51	82	479 (3)
After school detention	78	73	65	88	56	54	414 (5)
Lunchtime detention	48	38	32	49	13	25	205 (7)
Sent to Head of Year or Department Head	94	84	79	60	75	78	470 (4)
Removal of privilege	39	44	18	38	33	21	193 (8)
Given lines	18	15	20	20	3	9	85 (12)
Told off privately	52	29	37	21	23	30	192 (9)
Sent out of class	48	43	50	40	30	43	254 (6)
Moved seats	31	33	35	22	16	14	151 (11)

Many schools now use our system of a visual warning card similar to the yellow card in football. When the pupil breaks one of the codes of conduct, they are quickly issued with a warning card on the desk beside them and told which behaviour is unacceptable and the rule that it breaks. If the pupil chooses to continue to break the rule, they receive a sanction. If they choose to change their behaviour and return to task, the warning is removed and the pupil has a 'clean slate' again. This system cuts out much of the futile debate about whether pupils did or did not deserve the punishment just issued; did or did not hear the warning that was given, were or were not to blame for the incident. It also makes it possible to issue warnings to any of the people implicated in the incident. If they are innocent, they will return to task and have the warning removed.

In our experience, schools that build relationships need less sanctions

In my English lessons I've found a lot of the Circle Time techniques useful. Middle and low sets frequently resort to insult in dealing with each other. Circle Time cuts right through this and allows poor listening or behaviour to be dealt with immediately and crucially, calls for immediate improvement in behaviour in order to have the warning card removed. Although very strict rules are continually applied, they are used in a very non-confrontational way. I very rarely raise my voice or give detentions for behaviour now. Another bonus is that I am able to use pupils as models of good listening, reflection or concentration and praise it publicly and immediately. There is no time lag as in marking a book. Similarly pupils reward each other's by listening or picking an aspect of another's behaviour or work to praise. Many classes even bust into spontaneous applause now!

(Dominic Salles, English teacher)

The Elton Report (1989) highlighted that: 'The most effective sanction is the withdrawal of a privilege.' In primary school it is relatively easy to give children privilege time and then withdraw it a bit at a time if they fail to keep the golden rules. The challenge is to find ways of achieving the same effect at secondary school.

Here are some ideas that have been tried out by secondary teachers

- **Pupils can finish a few minutes early so that they leave exactly on time in order to be first in line for the lunch queue, or break. Everyone who has kept the rules during the lesson automatically has the privilege. Those who have broken a rule have been warned, then lose the privilege time in minute slots. They have to sit watching a sand timer (for years 7 and 8) while their class leaves.**
- **If everyone keeps the rules, the class can play a five-minute game at the end of the lesson.**
- **In Francis Coombe School, the Head of Year 7 allows all year 7 pupils who have kept the rules all week, to go home half an hour early on a Friday. The others have to stay.**
- **In special needs, it is possible to structure privileges much more tightly in order to guarantee success.**

8 Setting up a lunchtime policy

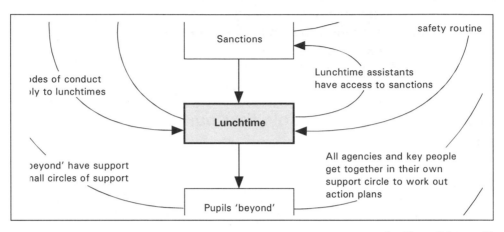

See Figure 2.1, page 12

When young people are asked about the part of the school day that causes them the most anxiety, lunchtimes feature highly. In fact, much of the trouble in schools comes from unstructured and poorly supervised time.

Behaviours that arise are:

- **fighting;**
- **bullying;**
- **bored behaviours (including smoking, drinking, drugs and going off-site);**
- **vandalism.**

Yet how much time is spent on INSET, policy development or inspection of lunchtimes? Schools cannot have policies based on respect if they commit the disrespect of abandoning pupils to their fate at lunchtime without structure or support. What are the messages of the hidden curriculum in relation to lunchtime? Similarly, what happens to pupils with special educational needs (SEN) at lunchtime? Does the school discontinue its caring policy for the hour and abandon young people to an unsupervised, unstructured 'fate'?

The informal curriculum of the playground demonstrates interpersonal skills, creativity, conflict resolution, negotiation, leadership, teamwork, empathy and self-organisation. This is the place where skills learned in the formal curriculum are put into practice and new skills are developed. If in the classroom, behaviour is tightly controlled, e.g. by shouting and using sarcasm, young people feel disempowered. The danger is that they will then seize power back by bullying. For some pupils, stress is caused, not by being part of the incident, but by observing other people being hurt or misbehaving. When the experiences of lunchtime are frightening or hurtful, learning is impaired in the afternoon and it is not possible for pupils to achieve academic excellence.

Secondary schools need to address the important issues of a lunchtime policy. What are they doing to make lunchtimes emotionally and physically safe for all pupils? So many pupils are 'running scared'.

Pupils are not the only ones at risk however. Lunchtime policies also need to look at the staff. Are teachers too exhausted and stressed to teach well in the afternoon? The Lunchtime Report (Eurest 1997) showed that less than half of workers take a daily lunch break and 29 per cent claim never to take a lunch break. Even more worrying is that 83 per cent of workers say they do not have a drink during their lunch break either. Recent research is showing a link between mental health, stress and the immune system. People who manage their stress levels well by looking after their bodies, including eating well and taking a break in the middle of the day, have healthier immune systems and are less likely to have time off work. Calmer lunchtimes will lead to calmer, more productive afternoons.

So how do we go about making a lunchtime policy that works?

Ideas to consider

- Is there a regular review of the dining hall or canteen system and supervision? How orderly and efficient is the canteen system? Are the staff who supervise the canteen given respect by pupils? Are these staff supported by teaching staff?
- Is the playground divided into zoned areas for different activities? Are there separate areas in the outside area to accommodate pupils who want to play ball games or run around and those who want to sit and quietly chat?
- Is there any equipment available for activities to reduce boredom? So often the unacceptable behaviour encountered during lunchtime is the result of having nothing to do; it is bored rather than bad behaviour. Are there clubs and activities during lunchtime? Is there equipment that can be borrowed? Is there a common room that older pupils can use? Are there 'indoor' supervised clubs?
- Is there a football policy with equal opportunities and restricted areas for play? Football can so easily come to dominate the available space of a playground, particularly when grass areas are out of action in the winter.
- Are the moral rules that apply outside the school building the same as those that apply inside? Do the midday supervisors know the codes of conduct and have they received training in dealing with pupils who present challenging behaviour?
- Is there proactive work done to raise the status and power of midday supervisory staff?
- Do midday staff have access to photographs in order to identify pupils?
- Have you trained pupils as peer mediators for conflict resolution in the playground?
- Is there a clear policy on access to the buildings?
- Is there a clear policy on access to toilets?
- Is there a policy to build a sense of community through Circle Time and an active school council?

One way forward is to conduct an 'audit' of the school using questionnaires to all members of the school community including:

- senior managers
- teaching staff
- non-teaching staff
- newly qualified teachers
- midday supervisory assistants
- pupils
- parents

An example of a questionnaire is given in Appendix C but it is only designed to give an idea of the kind of questions that could be asked. Every school would have to design their own questionnaires, adapted to their unique situation and needs.

Once you have acquired a clear picture of the current situation, you will be able to devise a strategy for developing a lunchtime policy which addresses the most urgent needs first.

9 Pupils 'beyond'

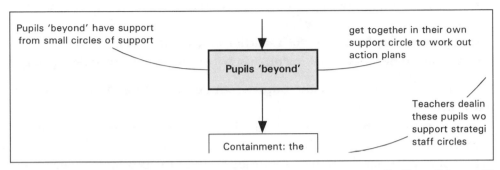

Pupils 'beyond' have support from small circles of support

get together in their own support circle to work out action plans

Pupils 'beyond'

Teachers dealin these pupils wo support strategi staff circles

Containment: the

See Figure 2.1, page 12

If you have ever had the opportunity to shadow a pupil in a secondary school, you will have discovered that pupils behave in different ways with different teachers. Simply calling behaviour 'disruptive' makes a value judgement but does not offer an accurate definition. Research by Daniels *et al.* (1999) on emotional and behavioural difficulties (EBD) in mainstream schools noted that staff could often make no clear distinction between low-level disruptive behaviour and true emotional behavioural difficulties. Those who did have an understanding of EBD recognised the causes to be complex and systemic involving home, school and less frequently biological factors. There was also an awareness that sometimes the behaviour of colleagues within the school could exacerbate pupils' difficulties. One teacher may ignore certain behaviour, while another may react in such a way that a major confrontation ensues. Jones (1980) offers a useful model to help understand the behaviour of young people with behavioural problems:

> In working with adolescents who are experiencing behaviour problems, I have consistently found that . . . within school, these adolescents fail to experience one or more of the essential ingredients of significance, power and competence . . . It is understandable that when adolescents are unable to meet these needs in socially acceptable ways they become involved in unacceptable behaviours.

An adoption of Jones' perspective highlights the need for a whole-school proactive approach to preventing disruption. In fact, without a whole-school approach that promotes a positive school environment, it becomes extremely difficult to identify pupils with emotional and behavioural difficulties. It is by devising and implementing systems that cater for the physical, emotional, social and learning needs of the majority that the minority who have more specific needs can be identified.

The Elton Report (1989) also drew attention to the need for a proactive approach to improving behaviour by highlighting the frustration and stress experienced by teachers dealing with children who have behavioural difficulties. It recommended that 'working towards a whole-school policy alongside helping individual teachers improve their group management skills can help many schools deal more effectively with the wide range of low-level disruptive incidents'.

It is not the low-level disruptive incidents that we are concerned with in this section, however. Pupils 'beyond' are those pupils whose behaviour is extremely challenging. We define 'pupils beyond' as those beyond all strategies outlined so far in our model. S/he is one who has been offered yet failed to respond to regular empathic listening opportunities and regular participation in Circle Time. S/he:

- **has a clear understanding of the codes of conduct expected by the school**
- **has received regular incentives;**
- **knows the safe boundaries of a sanction system that is respectful;**
- **is aware of negotiation taking place between the school and his/her parents.**

Despite all these measures, the pupil continues to adhere to disruptive, unhappy or withdrawn behaviour.

These pupils have become trapped in patterns of negative interaction with teachers and peers and exhibit behaviour consistent with their worldview. The behaviour we, as teachers, find so difficult serves the purpose of keeping the pupil's

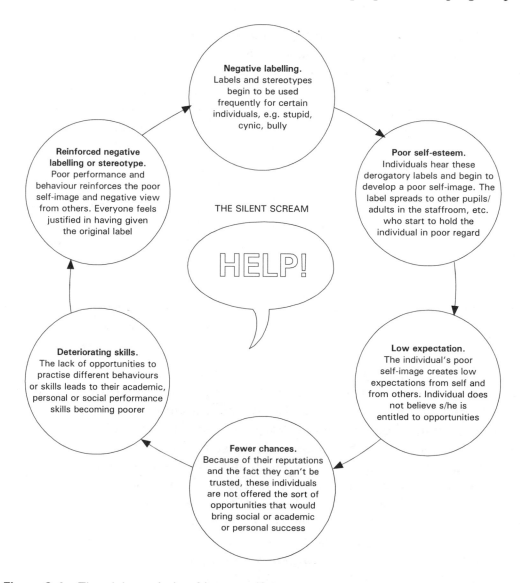

Figure 9.1 The vicious circle of lower self-esteem

inner world 'safe'. Often life has disempowered these young people, adults have let them down and many have been subjected to various arbitrary, confusing or outright abusive experiences. They become locked into a circle of negative self-esteem (Figure 9.1) and develop behaviours designed to protect and release their feelings in order to draw attention to their level of distress or anxiety. If other people fail to see beyond the behaviour and do not offer them in Rogers's words (1983) 'unconditional warmth and acceptance of the unique and good person they are meant to be' then they resort to negative behaviours as a way of receiving much-craved-for attention. Hostile attention is better than no attention.

The range of behaviours these young people exhibit are designed to hurt, anger or confuse people who come near them, thereby precluding any chance of their entering into a warm, reciprocal relationship with that person. Their behaviour keeps people at bay so, from their point of view, getting told off regularly means that at least they are the centre of someone's existence without being vulnerable to the hurt which may be incurred if they become involved in a positive relationship with them. Repetition of these behaviours then unconsciously and perversely means that they can regain a level of control over their lives and reduce levels of 'unsafety'.

To put it simply, if a young person with very low self-esteem is responded to in a warm and positive way, it can be a frightening experience. It challenges the person to take on a more positive view of him/herself and consider the possibility of involving him/herself in a relationship with another person. S/he then has to trust that this other person will sustain and nurture the positive experience. Trust is a risk-laden response. It is much safer to remain in control over your own world by not allowing yourself to enter into relationships. By refusing to change, the person refuses to hope and in this way remains in control. S/he my have a lot invested in staying negative.

Identifying and supporting pupils 'beyond'

I am sure that all teachers have at some time experienced aggressive and dismissive behaviours from pupils when they tried to praise or appreciate them. The paper containing the praised work may well be screwed up or defaced, the certificate torn or thrown away. I have known the work to hit one wall and the pencil another as the chair hit the floor! When pupils give aggressive, abusive and sometimes physically dangerous responses in the teacher–pupil relationship, the temptation is to give up on the whole notion of self-esteem. The truth is that people with low self-esteem are desperately difficult to reach. Success is hugely threatening to them so the pupils who most need us are most likely to repel us. Under these circumstances, even the kindest and most positive adults find it extremely difficult to carry on offering a warm, empathic relationship.

Support for adults

Figure 2.1 has an arrow from pupils 'beyond' back up to the listening systems because any member of staff who is dealing with these pupils needs the support of colleagues. They need a Circle Time to discuss issues and strategies for coping with challenging behaviour. They might also benefit from one-to-one peer support from a peer mentor who will listen effectively and provide a debrief session from time to time. In other contexts where adults deal with difficult behaviour such as mental aftercare, adults with learning disabilities or disadvantaged groups needing counselling, supervision is provided. Yet schools expect staff to cope with difficult and even abusive situations with no form of formalised support. The mental health of the staff has never been a priority in education.

Tiny, achievable, tickable targets (TATTs) may help

One method that is helpful in dealing with disturbed and disturbing pupils is to develop systems for focusing on and celebrating small moments of success. Guaranteeing daily success for the pupil with low self-esteem is very important if s/he is frightened to face its implications. Individually agreed contracts can be drawn up

Figure 9.2 Positive circle of higher self-esteem

that enable pupils to set realistic goals and be rewarded for small successes. The tutor, special needs coordinator and/or behavioural support staff meet with the pupil to negotiate and agree targets, which are within the pupil's capability. A motivational reward system is also negotiated with the pupil, while the key staff devise a method of keeping track of success throughout the school day. These systems require considerable liaison and agreement across curriculum areas in a secondary school, but where they are successfully implemented as part of a whole-school approach they are effective in creating and maintaining the positive school environment (Daniels *et al.* 1999: 82).

Intervention with tiny, achievable targets in any part of the negative cycle of poor self-esteem has the effect of breaking into the cycle and increasing the person's sense of worth and competence (Figure 9.2). The principle can be summed up as 'Catch them being good. Blink and you'll miss it!'

Introduce Circles of Support

There are times when a pupil's behaviour has gone well beyond the bounds of acceptable standards despite negotiated contracts and the introduction of a tiny, achievable, tickable targets scheme. These pupils need the opportunity to experience the support of a small circle in which to understand their own behaviour, to practise social skills and to develop alternative, positive ways of behaving. Mosley (1991) documented a case study of setting up and running a peer support group for helping disruptive and withdrawn pupils improve their self-concept by taking more responsibility for themselves.

Before the group could be set up, it was necessary to identify the behaviours that caused teachers the greatest anxiety. A wide range of teachers from the school were asked to provide a brief written statement describing, as accurately as possible, the pupil behaviours they found most disturbing. This resulted in a list of behaviours that naturally fell under three headings:

- *Behaviour characterised by lack of self-control:* **These behaviours were the most usual cause of anxiety. They involved activities such as shouting out, talking while the teacher is talking and stopping other pupils from working.**
- *Hostile behaviour:* **These behaviours were not as frequently mentioned but tended to be more pronounced in the upper school.**
- *Withdrawn behaviour:* **These behaviours tended to be overlooked and the teacher's attention had to be deliberately drawn to these pupils in order to produce a relevant list.**

(Appendix B shows a full list of the behaviours identified by the staff.)

The next task was to identify pupils in year 7 and 8 who were most frequently and similarly assessed by all their teachers as experiencing these behaviours and to interview them individually to find out if they found some of their school situations difficult and would like the opportunity to change their behaviour. 11 out of 13 pupils took up the offer of the peer support group.

The group met weekly for one hour. Each circle meeting followed the same four-part structure of discussion, warm-up, action and reflection. The content for discussion arose from the pupils' situations and current experiences and many of the issues were explored using a variety of role-play techniques. Each student was offered ten minutes' individual time after the circle to negotiate a contract of tiny achievable targets which they would take to their other subject lessons. Written and verbal evaluations from all the pupils, teachers and parents who took part in this educational programme testify to the improvements in these pupils' behaviour and relationships. They were helped to break out of the stereotyped image of the trouble-maker and see themselves as individuals capable of exploring and making changes in their lives. The circle was always run by two 'co-workers' so they support each other. One experienced circle facilitator and one head of year or key teacher make a good team and in this way you can help build teachers' group work skills.

Circles for case conferences

Another way of using the Circle Time model is to assemble all the people involved with a particular pupil and run a case conference as a circle-time meeting. The ground rules of respect enable each person to bring their perspective without fear of being interrupted or put down. The emotional safety generated by a circle meeting also facilitates separating issues from individuals so that people are less likely to become personal or defensive.

In summary

This model offers a range of proactive strategies including student-centred listening, behavioural rewards and sanctions, and the cognitive approaches of negotiated contracts and TATTs. It then supports the pupils at risk of disaffection by early intervention with peer support circles. If these systems are put in place as a long-term strategic policy starting with year 7, the numbers of pupils needing specialist EBD support would be greatly reduced. It is also likely that, as a result, there would be a happier school ethos, less absence and far fewer fixed term exclusions in the later years.

10 The containment stage or how do we cope when nothing works?

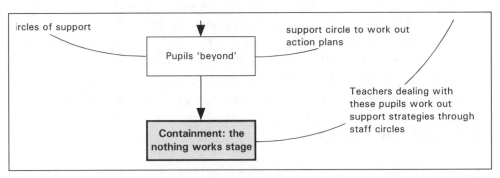

See Figure 2.1, page 12

'Containment' is implemented when nothing else works. At this stage we may be dealing with pupils who may have have deep pyschological, social, emotional problems. There can be within them a well of violence or self-destructive behaviour that needs only the smallest trigger such as a misplaced look. They are often at the very end of the road in mainstream education, and alternative provision is being considered for this pupil as the school has provided everything it can to help. You would need to be sure that you, as a school, could genuinely agree that this pupil:

- **has been offered at least one respectful, valuing relationship;**
- **knew one specific person was his/her advocate working on his/her behalf;**
- **had a clearly explained understanding of the codes of conduct and received lots of positive feedback through tiny targets linked to incentives;**
- **had been invited to support circles and slammed his/her way out, refusing the help that was offered;**

and that school liaison staff have visited his/her home (social worker, education welfare officer or health visitor) and there have been case conferences run as circles with the specialised agencies. Only then can you say you've reached the last stage in our model.

The reality of teaching is that it is not possible to meet the needs of every pupil and by this stage it is no longer acceptable to keep teachers and other pupils vulnerable to this level of disruption. It has become more important to consider how to 'contain' the disruptive pupil so that the class is not endangered by the threat of eruption.

Containment or effective damage limitation

Some schools have a sanctuary or 'time out' zone, monitored by key people where the pupil is kept 'off timetable' until a place can be obtained at the Pupil Referral

Unit or equivalent. If this is not possible, a 'help' system can be used. This involves 'training' a few pupils in each class to take a prearranged signal, such as a coloured card, to the office or staffroom. The timetable is arranged so that one senior member of staff is always available and on 'help duty' so that he or she can be contacted in the event of an emergency. This member of staff would be informed of the need for help in a particular room with a particular member of staff and would go to remove the pupil from the situation. The teacher's sanity is now of more importance than this pupil's education and it is imperative that we keep the situation in perspective.

As we said in the section on pupils 'beyond', the most important thing when dealing with extremely challenging pupils is to have staff circle meetings to discuss feelings and strategies. Often teachers become isolated, feeling that they are the only one who cannot handle this particular pupil. A 'safe' forum for discussing what does and does not help in the situation can be very therapeutic for the teacher and 'pooled' ideas or strategies help everyone who has to face difficult and highly disruptive behaviour on a daily basis.

Part II
The Practice

'There is no end to a circle or what can be done within it'
Urmila Ramakrishna

11 How to make Circle Time work

Having now unravelled the whole model, we need to move on to look at the role of Circle Time itself and how to run successful circles.

Initiatives for personal social education in secondary schools have regularly come, enjoyed a season of popularity and disappeared. Often this is because of new curriculum pressures, or teachers lose sight of the reasons for doing it. The practical difficulties of setting up the room or organising the activities can erode commitment to the process. Circle Time requires a degree of classroom reorganisation, which can prove daunting in the stresses of school life. One way of ensuring that it continues to happen is to involve the pupils in the physical organisation of the room. If it is treated like a military exercise with numbers under the desks and a master plan on the wall, pupils will join in the work involved in order to get the Circle Time that they enjoy. You, the classroom practitioner may well feel that this five minutes at the beginning and end of each lesson is wasted time. We would encourage you to run a series of six or seven weeks, review how much time is redeemed by pupils being involved in the lesson, 'on task' and not disrupting, then decide whether it is worth the time investment.

What are the ground rules that make Circle Time safe?

Probably the single most important factor in establishing Circle Time in the secondary school is emotional 'safety'. Is it 'safe' to speak or will someone shout me down? Will I be heard or will what I say be judged or brought up again at a future date? Once the group has agreed to abide by clear ground rules, it becomes 'safe' to talk and meaningful progress is made. Pupils of secondary age are often craving for a place in which to talk about issues that face them in school, at home and in their personal relationships. So in order for Circle Time to work everyone must be safe from:

- **overt criticism;**
- **mockery from anyone else;**
- **teacher's control techniques that involve 'showing pupils up'.**

Good communication only takes place in a climate of emotional 'safety'.
Teachers and pupils need to agree:

- **not to interrupt each other;**
- **to signal if you wish to speak;**

- not to use put-downs (either verbal or non-verbal) towards each other;
- if anyone does not wish to speak, he/she may say 'Pass';
- at the end of the round anyone who chose not to speak can be given a second opportunity;
- not to name anyone in a negative way. Instead they must say 'Someone constantly takes my equipment' or 'Some people push into the queue'. Similarly, the circle rules enable pupils to respect the privacy of their families. As in all situations when personal matters are being discussed, pupils must be reminded that if they want to tell you anything of a serious nature, they should use private, one-to-one time. Make sure that you warn pupils that if they ever choose to tell you anything through the listening systems that causes you concern, you may have to take it further.

How can I keep discipline during Circle Time?

One of the most frequently asked question when training secondary teachers in using Circle Time is 'How can I keep discipline? What do I do when a pupil will not keep the ground rules?' These questions are usually asked with particular characters in mind whom the teacher has found difficult in other lessons. The anxiety in taking on a new technique when the tried and tested ones are not working is understandable and the temptation is to stick with the familiar methods whether or not they are successful. This can lock both teacher and pupil into unhelpful cycles of action and response and serve to entrench the unwanted behaviour. Sometimes a new process such as Circle Time breaks the usual pattern of interpersonal relating and allows both parties to develop a different view of the other which in turn facilitates new ways of behaving.

We should right here and now say however, that Circle Time is not the 'instant cure' for pupils with emotional and behavioural difficulties and it does not immediately sort out the characters who crave attention and seize any opportunity to get it. The primary technique used during Circle Time is motivation by praise. The emphasis is on positive strategies alongside genuine respect and interest. Consequently, pupils learn that the way to get noticed is by keeping the ground rules. In the circle the teacher acts as a facilitator; he or she determines not to get 'hooked' into negative exchanges and to stick with the issues, not allowing the interaction to become personalised. Similarly, it helps to have a system of recognising those pupils who have kept the ground rules by issuing slips of paper at the end of the lesson to every pupil who has not received a warning. These say 'Well done for keeping the ground rules of respect for others'. They can then be taken and 'cashed in' for a merit or house point in the main school incentive system.

For some pupils, this is not enough, however. They are so skilled at winding up teachers and getting attention without entering positive relationship that in order to establish the ground rules and generate an emotionally 'safe' climate, teachers need to have a system of sanctions which can be used during Circle Time. If a pupil consistently breaks a ground rule a warning card (as discussed in Chapter 7) is placed at his/her feet in the circle. The ground rule is explained and the pupil is warned that if s/he continues to break the rule they will have to leave the circle. If the disruption is minor, the pupil can be asked to sit out of the next game and invited back once they have agreed to conform to the ground rules. If the disruption is more serious, some teachers make an agreement with the person in the room next door so that any disruptive pupil can go there with some prearranged work. Pupils who do not cope with a whole-class Circle Time become candidates for the smaller support circles described in Chapter 10, where they can receive additional help with social skills and build their self-esteem.

Keeping it going – some pointers

When personal and controversial issues are under discussion *warn* students only to say as much as they feel is 'safe'; i.e. be very sure from the beginning to tell them that *they* are in charge of the information they entrust to the whole group. They must realise that although confidentiality is encouraged it is not guaranteed. Therefore, if there's anything too personal or private which they feel they need to discuss further, suggest to them that they ask to see you for a private chat at a different time.

- **Make sure you vary the circle approach. It includes warm-ups, games, paired talking/ listening exercises, rounds, discussion and role-play.**
- **You must accept any contribution, however 'off beat' with great respect.**
- **Thank students for their contribution whenever possible.**
- **Value all opinions equally without betraying irritable body language.**
- **You only use a 'speaking object' for a round, when everyone is given an opportunity to speak, otherwise pupils indicate with a hand if they wish to contribute to an open discussion.**
- **You must not interrupt if a pupil is using the speaking object to talk. If you need to say something, you have to move across the circle, touch the object, apologise for interrupting, then say whatever it is you have to say.**
- **Do not automatically think you have the best answers. If, for example, a pupil asks for help during open forum, you should raise your hand and wait to be chosen, just like any other class member.**
- **Evaluate regularly (e.g. 'The most boring/interesting part of this group for me was . . .')**
- **Make sure you follow-up any injustices or things that are 'going wrong' for students. Circle-work must not exist in isolation. They will only learn to trust you if they perceive you as genuinely caring about their needs and being prepared to do something on their behalf. Any issues of concern that affect school management could be taken to a school council circle meeting. Representatives from the school council would then take pupils' issues to the management of the school.**
- **Make sure you take a few minutes to evaluate the session too. If possible set up some form of support with colleagues to discuss the issues that are raised.**
- **Although you obviously will take a serious approach to this sort of work, try to make sure that you include some fun and wherever possible end on a light-hearted note with a game.**

12 The structure of a circle meeting

As with all good group process, the circle meeting moves through three phases:

- **introductory phase which can include warm-up games and rounds;**
- **middle phase – open forum;**
- **closing phase which can include celebration of success and closing games or rituals.**

Introductory phase

The warm-up game is very important at the beginning of Circle Time. Many games and activities can be used to energise or warm-up the group. They are specifically designed to:

- **generate a sense of 'group' identity by provoking laughter, fun and relaxation;**
- **encourage pupils to value and respect each individual' s contribution;**
- **encourage emotionally 'safe' self-disclosure, the basis of empathetic understanding;**
- **link in to the affective realm and thereby cause cognitive understanding of social, learning and relating skills to be more effective because it is linked to an emotional experience;**
- **cause pupils to sit next to and work with new people for different activities, creating interaction between as many group members as possible;**
- **create the need for positive eye contact (one of the most significant features of relationship building) between group members.**

The key to a good warm-up is to make it comfortable for as many of the group as possible so that people do not feel threatened and withdraw, or are embarrassed by finding the activity childish or silly. The myth of 'age-appropriate' games and warm-ups should be dispelled, however. Activities need to be 'group-appropriate' and once you have started with a safe game that is guaranteed to succeed, you can move on to more adventurous ones. Once a group is confident with one another and with the teacher, there is virtually no game that they will not play, no matter how 'childish' they appear.

The warm-up period is very important at the beginning of the life of a group. With a new class of year 7 pupils, it might be advantageous to spend half the Circle Time meeting on warm-up games and exercises. Games, rounds and celebration will quickly establish the rules and build trust, cooperation and the sense of belonging. These are essential prerequisites for meaningful and purposeful open forum. Classes vary enormously in regard to the time it takes to create mutual respect, empathy and belonging.

Round

Soon after the initial activity it is useful to move into a round or some verbal activity that requires young people to listen to each other. During a round a 'speaking object' is passed round as a visual symbol signifying the right to speak and be heard. Any object can be used and often an object with significance to the group emerges such as a conch, a coloured ceramic egg or a pebble. Whoever is holding the object has the right to speak without being interrupted. When s/he has finished talking, s/he passes the object on to the next pupil. In order to keep up a good pace and stop the circle 'grinding to a halt' with the vociferous dominating discussion, rounds are usually scripted with a sentence stem such as 'I don't like it when . . .'. The majority of people contribute to a round but anyone can say 'Pass' and hand the object on. The pupil who started the round will ask, at the end, if anyone who passed would like a turn to speak now. Every contribution is acceptable and valued, creating a climate of trust and genuine interest.

With groups of older pupils, especially when the group is newly formed, rounds can be used as a warm-up to the rest of the group activities. Sometimes it is helpful to put the group into pairs so that they discuss an issue with one other person before the round. This is much less threatening than launching into a personal statement in front of the whole group. A paired exercise can be followed by a round with 'I' statements or the pair can introduce one another and speak for their partner.

Partnerships for paired exercises need to be constantly changing in order to create new friendships and relationships and a maximum sense of 'group'. Using a game that causes people to change seats or mixing activities will change the pairs. Another method of mixing up the group is to give each group member the letter 'A' or 'B'. The 'A's talk to 'B's and after each paired activity, all the 'A's move on to the second, fourth or sixth chair along, so creating new pairs and groups.

Rounds can be as imaginative and as varied as you like. They can relate to the topic to be discussed in Open Forum or they can be for getting to know group members better by encouraging self-disclosure. Rounds can foster imagination and straightforward communication. They encourage empathy by opening up alternative ways of responding to the same question and assertiveness by the use of 'I' statements.

The most straightforward rounds relate to expressing feelings and associating them with cause or effect. In PSHE lessons, the rounds are related to the topic under discussion this week. Rounds are used any time opinion is sought or for evaluation and feedback.

Middle phase – open forum

This phase is the open-ended central focus that lies at the heart of Circle Time. Sometimes discussion starters and open questions will be posed during open forum that relate to PSHE topics. At other times it can consist of asking if there is anyone who needs help (this could refer to help with behaviour, curriculum, community issues, understanding global issues and so on). Drama techniques such as role-play are extremely helpful in this phase of Circle Time as this is the phase that most powerfully encourages pupils to develop 'inner locus of control', as discussed in Chapter 1.

Open forum is the most vulnerable to misuse by teachers and pupils and it is particularly important to keep people emotionally 'safe'. The three specific strategies for promoting emotional 'safety' in this model of Circle Time have already been mentioned in different places in this book. We will summarise them again for convenience:

1. **The teacher makes sure that s/he maintains a very** *positive attitude* **to the group. S/he models and insists that group members use positive communication including basic counselling skills and very good listening skills. The conditions that research has shown to be necessary for a person to risk changing their self-concept are respect, empathy, warmth and acceptance. The 'climate' in the group must be non-judgmental and accepting. Shouting out and interrupting are unacceptable.**

2. *No* **group member may use a** *name negatively.* **Nobody should ever be named, blamed or shamed during Circle Time. Names of parents, siblings, peers and teachers are not allowed. The individual says 'Someone is . . .' or 'People are . . .'. Another forum must be established where pupils can talk about individuals that are causing them a problem, so that the circle becomes a place where there is no risk of being shown up or picked on.**

3. *Scripts, sensitive discussion* **or** *drama approaches* **can be used during open forum. If pupils are being encouraged to ask for help with their behaviour, the script is 'Does anyone need help with their behaviour?' This encourages the notion that we all need some help with our behaviour at one stage or another in life. It also promotes responsibility for owning the need to ask for help when you need it. Throughout the process of asking for and receiving helpful suggestions for resolving problems, the person seeking help has control over the process, s/he can choose to do something about the behaviour or problem, or choose not to, but the responsibility is left with the individual. S/he cannot blame other people for the behaviour. When offering help or advice to a member of the group who has asked for it, group members say 'Would it help if I . . . ?' or 'Would it help if you . . . ?' or 'Would it help if we . . . ?'. The person who has asked for help responds to each suggestion, first by thanking the person who offered the help and then by either accepting or rejecting it, e.g. 'Thank you, but I don't think that will help because I've tried it before . . .' or 'That sounds like a good idea. I'll try that. Thank you.'**

It is astonishing how generous and helpful even the most difficult group of pupils can become when open forum is structured in this way. They also learn how to understand another person's view of a situation (empathy) and how to deal with other people in a non-confrontational way.

From the open-forum discussion, the individual or the whole group devise an action plan of possible ways forward, which promotes personal and group responsibility for behaviour and actions. As with every action plan, it needs to be reviewed after an agreed time.

The open forum may not need to be as highly structured as outlined above. During this time, it is possible to introduce various techniques including role-play, scripted drama, discussion and brainstorming. One particularly useful drama technique is 'doubling'. The drama can be 'frozen' at any stage and members of the circle are encouraged to stand beside an 'actor', putting a hand on one of his/her shoulders and speaking their thoughts aloud. Similarly, group members can stand beside the official player and give an alternative script so that the group receives a variety of views on possible outworkings of the role-play. The main concern is to find ways to help people share each other's dilemmas and deepen their empathy. Therefore it is better to de-emphasise the audience role by introducing a range of strategies to encourage participation by all group members. As we run circles all over the country, we are constantly amazed at the level of sensitive, generous, creative thinking that young people invest in helping one another during this part of Circle Time.

Closing phase

It's important to help group members to move away from the issues of concern raised in the middle phase. They need a series of activities that lighten the mood and return safely to warm and positive experiences. This can be achieved by encouraging pupils to thank group members for their contribution to the group dynamics. Any member of the group can nominate another to be thanked, e.g. a quiet member of the group, or a member with a good sense of humour etc. This activity involves one-to-one positive and direct communication. It is to do with giving and receiving compliments and is an important component of building self-esteem and positive relationships. One word of warning for teachers is that some pupils will be constantly left out of a spontaneous session of 'thank yous' so that sometimes is it good to generate situations that enable the least popular group members to receive thanks. Whatever your strategy, see this as a winding-down phase which, to achieve a proper feeling of closure, will need an ending ritual. This could include some form of reflection or a game to engender laughter or provide a 'bridge' into the next activity of the day. A useful closure might be a quick round of 'One thing I am looking forward to today is . . .'.

The skills for learning and relating

Throughout all circle-time activities run the skills of looking, listening, speaking, thinking and concentrating. These are the skills required for learning and for forming good relationships. In order to teach young people the processes of learning and relating these skills need to be made explicit by drawing attention to them as they are used or required in games and activities.

For instance, when pupils are asked to work in groups, sometimes the work can be prefaced by a short discussion on what makes groupwork difficult or easy, or a round of 'I find groupwork difficult when . . .'. Once people have reflected on the processes of groupwork and their own contribution to it, plus they have heard how actions affect other people, they can begin to take responsibility in regulating their own behaviour in order to make groupwork more productive and satisfying for everyone. This process of reflection can apply to any skill area and the skills themselves can be practised and discussed explicitly. The highlighting and discussion of skills has been left out of all the outlines for circle sessions in Part IV but the more practised the teacher-facilitator becomes, the more they will draw attention to the skills and processes that underpin this kind of groupwork.

13 Case studies and glimpses of Circle Time practice

We asked a number of teachers who have been involved in using Circle Time in a variety of contexts to give their opinion on its value.

Implementing Circle Time as a tutor

Caroline Atherton, Cranford Community School

I began using Circle Time in registration with year 7 groups. I ran six 20-minute sessions and included themes of friendship, cooperation, the community, feelings and self-awareness. Even in these short sessions the tutors and myself have noticed an increase in self-confidence of some students . . . It is intended that tutors will continue to use Circle Time with their tutor groups throughout their school lives, thus providing them with a forum for problem-solving and building self-confidence.

Esther de Burgh Thomas, Islington Comprehensive

Esther watched a demonstration of Circle Time and attended a training session before trying out the strategies herself. She found two secrets to making Circle Time work.

The first secret is the huge difference that can be made by positive discipline. We have all heard this buzzword, so to make the concept more real to you here are some of the ways positive language is used in Circle Time.

And you're putting your hand up, which really helps me . . . That was good listening . . . At least you know it (to a boy who said he deliberately annoys his teachers) – a lot of people don't know it . . . You owned up to a lot of things – your honesty is one of your strong qualities.

During Circle Time demonstrations, as an observer, I watched as this ongoing positive script transformed a very average class into a hardworking, considerate and sensitive self-help group. Even a notoriously boisterous year 7 class in an Islington comprehensive became eager to please and extraordinarily sensitive to each other's needs.

I have had to work very hard at remembering to be positive with my own form. It's not easy to break the pattern of a lifetime especially when one's form knows (or thinks they know) what to expect from one and are suspicious of any newly adopted style. As if this isn't enough to contend with, there is the tiredness factor, peculiar to all the state schools I have worked in. The word 'don't' can trip all-too-easily from the lips in these moments of exhausted weakness. The best way to avoid the tiredness trap is to make a conscious effort to counteract it. In order to be as positive as possible (which should be done before any circle-time session, even if it means 30 seconds standing in the corridor telling yourself you are happy and relaxed). I recommend five minutes sitting on your own.

Tiredness aside, it is more effective to praise the ones being good than focusing on those that are less cooperative. Positive discipline will, in the long run not only save you energy but also *give* you energy as your pupils go out of their way to get you to give them yet more positive feedback.

The second secret is the games. As to which games are played during Circle Time, it doesn't matter as long as they are short (between three and five minutes). If in doubt as to what game to play, ask your pupils – they will have vivid memories of organised games from primary school days and will be happy to share their expertise with you. After a quick game a pupil is so alert and ready for action that he cannot help but be tuned in to the whole-class conversation that follows. Games are an experiential way of teaching pupils rules such as gentleness, kindness, hard work, turn taking, honesty and skills such as looking, listening, thinking, speaking and concentrating.

When I began to use games within Circle Time I allowed the games to go on for too long – the focus has to be the circle-time discussions because these can make such a huge difference to children's emotional lives. So five minutes is an absolute maximum for games. The reason I treasure the above two 'secrets' is that the principles they are based on are universally applicable. They have wrought a transformation over the way I work and the way I feel about children.

Jennie Burley, Head of DT and a tutor, Dorset

Circle Time was used with a year 10 tutor group where there was evidence of a group pressurising an individual. The class used the drama studio for the circle and it gave tutees an opportunity to speak and be listened to. They shared their feelings without embarrassment and allowed those who did not want to speak to pass. The group felt secure, confidentiality was maintained and it helped in clarifying and setting about resolving the problem.

Promoting Quality Circle Time in our school

Isobel McFarlane, Inverkeithing High School

I became interested in Circle Time initially through my involvement in the Area Group (the high school and its six feeder primaries) and a long-term interest I have always had in primary/secondary transfer. I have certainly been concerned that, in spite of making great strides forward in primary–secondary liaison, we still have a huge gulf between the ethos of a primary and that of a secondary. Given the sheer size of our school (1400 pupils)

Sue Chudley, Head of Girls' PE and a tutor, Dorset

I used Circle Time with a new PSE group. We moved the tables and made a large circle of chairs. The topic was talking to new people and ways of making people feel good by our comments. A soft ball was used to ensure that everyone had the opportunity to speak. (It also gave the nervous something to fiddle with and squeeze!) The pupils said how nice it was to have something good said about them, especially first thing in the morning. The attributes others acknowledged in them were often ones they had never thought of, e.g. hair looked nice, always smiling, never put others down etc. Despite it being a new concept, everyone enjoyed it.

things are bound to be different. But I have long felt that we should be doing more to provide continuity and progression in the hidden curriculum and in approaches to discipline as well as across all the modes. It seemed to me that our primary schools to a greater or lesser degree were committed to Circle Time but it all stopped when the pupils crossed the high-school threshold.

So far I have used Circle Time with my first year Personal and Social Education class. I have also, as an experiment used Circle Time with a difficult third year group whom the teacher had to come to me for help with. This was a learning experience for me and while the class and the teacher were enthusiastic about the session I had my reservations. However, I learned a lot from it. I have used the warning cards with various classes to great effect.

Quality Circle Time is a great means of delivering the PSE programme where above all we are trying to create a climate of mutual trust and raise self-esteem with golden rules to encourage self-respect. A dream of mine would be to have a suitable room designated for Circle Time – look out for low-flying pigs!!! I loathe having to talk to children about personal issues with them stuck behind desks. Unfortunately many classrooms in secondary do not lend themselves to arranging a circle (fixed benches in Science for example). PSE tends to be timetabled after the academic subjects so it's whatever rooms are left that are designated for PSE. Added to that, some of the teachers who deliver the PSE programme are 'conscripts' and not volunteers. However, I am hopeful that through in-service I can introduce Circle Time in PSE and encourage staff to overcome the difficulties in less than suitable classrooms.

It is difficult to envisage how the whole quality circle model could be introduced into secondary. Certainly golden rules displayed throughout the school would be great but it would be difficult for example to introduce a privilege on a regular basis given the pressure on staff to complete a course when they only see the class for perhaps 2–4 periods per week. It would be particularly difficult given the time pressures of the Standard Grade and Higher curriculum. Here we have introduced in the past year 'Recognised Achievement' certificates for 1st and 2nd year pupils. These certificates are awarded annually with a trip in the summer term for those who are awarded two certificates. Although recognising that rewarding good behaviour is a major step forward, from my point of view the difficulty with this is, as you know, asking some pupils to behave for a whole term is almost impossible. They need much more achievable targets with regular rewards (like weekly Golden Time provides in primary).

Using Circle Time for primary 7 to senior form 1 transition work

Edith Forrest, Behaviour Support, Perth and Kinross

I am working with a Primary 7 class of children with social/emotional difficulties at Northern District School, Perth. It was felt that the children would benefit from small support circles prior to coming together for Circle Time.

Currently there are three groups of children following the same Circle Time cooperative skills programmes which have been pre-planned by the members of staff leading the groups (Building Bridges Project). The programmes are focused on identifying feelings in themselves and others and incorporating this into a problem-solving model.

The groups will continue until Easter, then amalgamate for Circle Time in the summer term. At this point Circle Time will be used specifically as a forum to address the children's concerns about moving to secondary school.

Members of the secondary staff (Guidance and Support for Learning) will attend Circle Times to answer the children's questions and respond to their concerns. They also wish to become experienced in the structure and language of Circle Time, in order to continue it in secondary and support other colleagues in doing so.

Pupils from the secondary school will join us to give peer support through Circle Time.

Finally we hope to be able to run a Circle Time for the children in their secondary school before the summer holiday so that they know there is a listening system for them in their new school.

Mandy Robinson, Head of RE and a tutor, Dorset

I used Circle Time with a year 10 PSE group that was new to me. I felt that I usually talked too much during these lessons and I wanted a way of getting them all to have a say, not just the vociferous. We moved the tables to the edge of the room and sat in a fairly cramped circle in the middle. I found that the group was not as chatty as I would have liked. Some were patently dumbstruck with this new technique. After all, they had already experienced three years of letting the noisy answer all the questions. Some found it hard to think of any positive aspects of themselves. They were much better at finding other people's good points. It 'broke the ice' and some seemed to appreciate the chance to speak. I'll need to work at this in order to get a freer exchange of opinions.

I also used Circle Time for a year 7 PSE lesson on loss and change at the beginning of the spring term. We were looking back at changes, especially in friendship groups since starting at secondary school and will move on from loss of friends to bereavement. We passed a purple egg and any pupils who wanted to speak held the egg and finished the sentence 'My friends have changed because . . .'. Virtually every child spoke and the couple of boys who chose not to say anything passed the egg with an embarrassed laugh. Two main themes emerged, firstly the loss of junior school friends and secondly, making new friends. I shared the loss of my former tutor group that I had had for five years. It did not seem like a PSE *lesson*, more an exchange of shared experiences. Children who do not normally volunteer to speak felt 'safe' to do so and the sharing helped us to become a more cohesive group.

Case Study

**Ann Boardman, South Essex Health Authority and
Norma Cox, Tameside Community Care Trust, South Essex**

While working as health promotion specialists in South Essex we became aware that primary schools in our area were increasingly using Circle Time as an approach to school management, behaviour management and delivery of many areas of the National Curriculum, including PSHE. Many schools were recognising the potential of this approach for development of the competencies associated with mental well-being and the crucial links between mental well-being and effective learning.

The National Health Service Advisory Service suggest competencies should include:

- **the ability to develop psychologically, emotionally, intellectually and spiritually;**
- **the ability to initiate, develop and sustain mutually satisfying relationships;**
- **the ability to become aware of others and to empathise with them;**
- **the ability to use psychological distress as a development process so that it does not impair further development (HMSO 1995).**

A number of Circle Time models have been developed over the past 15 years. In south Essex, we found considerable support amongst local advisors, head teachers and special educational needs coordinators for the Jenny Mosley Quality Circle Time Model. This model was considered to provide a psychologically and philosophically well-structured practical strategy which can be embraced by a whole-school community so that the mental well-being of every child, every member of staff and every member of the school community is enhanced.

Similar approaches are also being developed in the United States for the development of emotional literacy (Goleman 1996). The programmes featured in many such models are strikingly similar to the UK models as are the outcomes, including widespread benefits for children's emotional and social competence, for their behaviour in and out of the classroom and for their ability to learn. Goleman also advocates the use of such approaches during periods of transition, for example for pupils moving from one phase to another.

As Circle Time becomes more widely used in primary schools in south Essex we realised that young people entering secondary schools will increasingly expect such a forum to be available to them. Consequently we have started to explore the potential for introducing quality Circle Time to secondary schools in south Essex.

To advance our exploration of the potential use of Circle Time in secondary schools, teachers from health promoting schools in south-east Essex were invited to participate in an INSET day. Before the INSET, senior secondary staff thought Circle Time was essentially a primary strategy with no relevance to the secondary context. After participating in the training day some teachers took the ideas away to use in their secondary schools. They have started to use Circle Time with a variety of groups:

- **pupils on an Alternative Education Programme;**
- **to investigate barriers to revision with a GCSE group;**
- **for year 7 pupils to foster a sense of community as they enter the secondary school.**

Case Study

Possible ways forward for using Circle Time
Sam Butler, Acting Head of Year 8, Sheoburyness County High School

Shoeburyness County High School have been looking at ways of implementing the Whole School Quality Circle Time Model and adapting it to their situation. Their thinking to date is summarised in the following bullet points:

- Pupils identified with manifesting behavioural problems to meet regularly for Circle Time. However if this strategy were to be adopted solely for pupils with behavioural difficulties, there would be a danger of its being regarded as having limited value elsewhere. It could be argued that other pupils would not appreciate its value for them and see it as something the pupils with 'special needs' do, making it difficult to implement across the entire school at a later stage. It is considered better to adopt Circle Time right across the school so that all pupils have access to it.
- During form period, time could be allocated for Circle Time to take place once a week and a skeleton agenda or selection of relevant pastoral tasks could be provided. There is also the scope for any issues which have arisen that week to be addressed.
- During form period, some time could be allocated for the form to have a circle discussion of School Council issues.
- During the allocated PSHE lesson, the School Council representatives could use a circle discussion to explore the issues raised by their year groups.
- One-to-one tutor time – perhaps year 7 and 8 could have a big ear on the board and they could put a small mouth on it when they want to speak to their form tutor privately. Older pupils could have an appointment system where they put their names – similar to a business diary.
- The one-to-one tutor time would give pupils an appropriate time to speak with their form tutor and thus would hopefully prevent sensitive personal issues being divulged to the class inappropriately during Circle Time.
- Teachers could be made aware, if not already, of using the circle as another teaching strategy. The more teaching strategies we have the better.
- Each term a department could be responsible for arranging a staff event, e.g. a meal, go-kart racing, bowling etc. The whole school's staff would be invited. The activities should suit all members of staff, especially those with significant home commitments. Friday night down the pub, important though this activity is, unfortunately doesn't include everyone.
- Each member of staff throughout the school to have a 'buddy'.
- Each member of staff to have a 'peer support system' to turn to in moments of need and for this to be non-judgemental.
- Perhaps during INSET to have more time specifically spent on the staffs' mental health, e.g. sessions on dealing with stress and managing difficult pupils.
- The model is built upon 'Personal Mental Health Plans' for all staff which is good for all concerned. It invests in the staff and tries to raise self-esteem among the staff. This investment has the potential to help increase the staff morale and thus the standard of teaching, not only during Circle Time but for the majority of their teaching as well.
- A pilot system could he introduced to assess the scheme's potential.

Using Circle Time in an Alternative Education Programme

Mary Bright, Alternative Education Programme, Shoeburyness County High School

The primary aim of alternative education is to raise the self-esteem of pupils who see themselves as failures and thus reject school. Building relationships is our first task. Many of the pupils we work with have a high level of frustration and show little understanding or tolerance to others in the group. Their comments can be vitriolic and damaging. Physical assaults and threats are not unusual.

In tutor period we work very hard to reverse the ingrained negative responses. Developing social skills underpins all aspects of the course and Circle Time has been an excellent vehicle for this. We began by discussing positive aspects about ourselves, i.e. 'One thing I'm pleased about . . .'. In the group this year, the girls have enjoyed the opportunities to explore ideas, but for several weeks the boys would simply opt out. This went on until one of the girls suddenly said 'They're out of order. They never say anything.' The rest of the girls joined in at this point and passed the card to John. Faced with this female solidarity, eyes down, John said 'I've been here for 100 per cent this term and I'm proud of myself'. A round of applause from the girls! Since then we seem to have broken the ice and it is OK for the boys to join in although they are still not as voluble as the girls.

I use Circle Time every two or three weeks to discuss relationships within the group, problems and difficulties and to celebrate success. It has been very useful to raise issues that would otherwise probably lead to a one-to-one confrontation. We have been able to deal with things by mutual agreement rather than teacher directives, which anyway don't work with pupils like these. Their response to difficult situations is to walk out of school and not come back. Circle Time has enabled us all to work things through together and develop bonds in the group. We still have our moments, like every day, but the difference in attendance, attitudes and goodwill is palpable. A number of tutors in year 7 have also started to use Circle Time.

> In our group we have used Circle Time for us to be able to talk to each other as a group one at a time when we get the card. We do this mainly because half of us have no confidence in ourselves and it helps us out of our shells. I felt that it helped me to get my opinion across to other people. (Female, 16 years)

> In our group we sometimes use Circle Time. It's been interesting and helpful because boys find talking and discussing things very hard. (Male, 16 years)

Part III

Activities, games, rounds, drama approaches and quizzes

How to use this section

This part of the book firstly presents whole circle-time lessons, allowing the reader an opportunity to use the material straight from the book. The circle-time lesson plans provide material for opening activities, rounds, games and open forum. They often only give the title of the games used, however, as these are detailed in the relevant sections that follow. Each circle-time script comes with a variety of ways of varying or extending it, including questions that the group can explore under open forum. As you become more confident, you will be able to let the group indicate the discussion that is relevant to them. Sections on games and activities, rounds, drama approaches and quizzes follow the circle-time lessons. These are presented in a mix and match form so you can select material suitable to the skills you wish to develop, or the topics you wish to cover.

Games are universal. Many of them are built into the folklore of society so we don't know who invented them. You will find familiar games in the selection provided and you will develop your own variations with the groups you teach. Games adapt to the social realities of the groups that play them and the art of using games is to live with the uncertainty of not knowing how any game or ensuing discussion might turn out.

Some of the games have been included simply to be played and enjoyed. Others have been included to provide a basis for further thought and discussion. They offer an ideal starting point for participants to consider some of the important issues in life and to discuss their own areas of concern. Many of the drama activities offer participants the opportunity to explore real-life problems and practise alternative ways of responding. While in the safe environment of the group, they can explore how to resolve issues in a more positive way. Pupils are encouraged to learn more about other people's behaviour and to acquire sensitivity, empathy and tolerance through understanding.

For each game, activity, drama strategy or quiz, there is a 'What to do' section which outlines the method of implementation, followed by 'How this could be varied or developed', which details either follow-on activities or ideas for discussion depending on the activity involved. The activities are presented in a planned and formal way. As you become more confident, it is vital that you adopt your own creative, 'free-wheeling' attitude towards them. Each session usually lasts from 40 minutes to an hour. If your time allocation is shorter, feel free to select activities and ideas that are most appropriate to the needs of your class. We do, however, advocate that you stick to the basic structure for circle-time sessions given in Chapter 11.

14 Circle scripts

This chapter presents an outline for 10 possible circle sessions.

Circle sessions on 'Who I am'

The pupils might like to create personal folders or large display charts about themselves.

Circle sessions on 'My social world'

Session 1   A personal profile

Materials

- clip boards
- personal profile sheets
- pencils

- prepared stick-on labels of famous people

Warm-up phase

The teacher has a prepared selection of the names of famous people (*which the pupils are likely to know*) written on stick-on labels, e.g. pop stars, film stars, well-known historical figures, television figures (these can include cartoon figures, e.g. Bart Simpson). The teacher sticks a label on to the back of each pupil and the participants circulate and question one another about their 'names' until they guess who they are. If there are a few left at the end who are having difficulty discovering who they are the teacher can call the class to order and the other pupils can offer them clues as to their identity.

Draw out the rules of no 'put-down', unkind laughter or ridicule about 'characters'.

Paired exercise

Discuss each other's 'characters' and find out one piece of information about each one.

Round

Each pupil says which famous person they are and one thing about him/her.

Sentence stem: 'I'm . . . and I . . .'

Personal profiles

Participants sit in a circle and are given pencils and personal profile sheets to complete. (See Figure 14.1 for an example of a personal profile sheet.)

Middle phase – open forum

The teacher facilitates a sensitive discussion about the personal profile sheets. Do they give a good idea of what you are like? What else might be added to the list? Did you find any sentence difficult to complete and, if so, why? Did you enjoy doing this exercise? Why can it be helpful to think about yourself in this way, especially focusing on the positive aspects? Do you sometimes forget the good things about yourself? When does this happen? Does anyone in the group feel bad about who they are at present and would anyone like some advice and suggestions on how to think more positively?

Scripts

'I need help because I feel . . .'   'Would it help if I . . .?'

'Would it help if you . . .?'   'Would it help if we . . .?'

Celebration

Is there anyone you would like to thank because their presence makes a positive contribution to the class? Say specifically what they do, e.g. smile a lot, stay calm etc.

Ending activity

Around the circle, each pupil in turn completes the sentence, 'One reason that I am glad to be who I am is . . .'

A personal profile of _____

My favourite book is _____

My favourite food is _____

My favourite TV programme is _____

My favourite pop group is _____

My favourite activity is _____

My favourite place is _____

My best holiday was at _____

One thing I don't like is _____

One thing I am good at is _____

The thing I like most about my appearance is _____

The thing I like least about my appearance is _____

One annoying habit I have is _____

A person (past or present) I really admire is _____

I really like it when _____

The nicest thing that happened to me was _____

My first memory is _____

My best subject at school is _____

One thing I'm afraid of is _____

My best quality is _____

One thing I'm not good at is _____

I believe that _____

One thing I hope for the future is _____

My main ambition is _____

I don't feel confident when _____

I used to worry about _____

My friends like me because _____

One thing I know a lot about is _____

One thing I'd like to learn about is _____

Figure 14.1   Personal profile sheet

Session 2 My life

Materials

- **a long sheet of paper for each pupil**
- **pens**
- **pencils**
- **rulers**

Warm-up activity

Using the initials of their first and surnames, the pupils have to respond to questions asked by the teacher. This can be done around the circle.

Examples

> Sasha Dempsey, what is your favourite food?
> Sasha could answer 'Soggy dough' or 'Sausage delight' or 'Sizzling dumplings' or 'Spam dinners'.

> Jason Connor, where would you like to go on holiday?
> Jason could answer 'Juvenile camp' or 'Jolly Canada' or 'Jousting centres'.

If the teacher has a selection of six or seven simple questions, they can be rotated. Alternatively s/he might ask the same question around the circle. Answers can be silly or nonsensical.

Life lines

Each pupil is given a sheet of paper and writing implement; rulers can be shared. They are instructed to draw a life line and fill in the positive and negative events of their lives (see page 95).

Paired activity

Create new pairs by asking pupils to 'move to a new chair if':

- **'You found it easy to draw your life line.'**
- **'You found happy events came to mind first.'**
- **'You found it easier to remember the sad/difficult events than the happy events.'**

Open forum

Pupils are asked to look over their life lines and the teacher facilitates an open discussion using questions such as: what makes life events positive or negative? Could other people see any of the events in a different way? What usually causes negative events? For example, chance, other people, changing circumstances, accidents, illness. Do they consider their lives have been generally happy or unhappy? Do they think people tend to remember good or bad events most or does it depend on the individuals concerned? Did anyone find it really difficult to remember positive events in their life? Can negative events ever have a positive outcome?

Celebration

Is there anyone in this class you want to thank because they are willing to try out new ideas and be adventurous?

Closing activity

Each pupil in turn completes the sentence 'One positive event I would like to see on my life line in the future is . . .'.

Session 3   Strengths and weaknesses

Materials

- strengths and weaknesses questionnaire
- pencils

Warm-up activity

Pupils sit in a circle. One chair is removed and pupil without chair stands in centre. The teacher calls out different categories. Any pupil who thinks s/he fits into the named category changes seat and the pupil standing in the centre tries to sit on a vacant chair. The pupil who is left without a seat stands in the centre until the next category is called. Once the game is established, the pupil in the middle can choose the next category.

Examples

Anyone who likes *EastEnders*.

Anyone who travels to school by bus.

Anyone who can do a headstand.

Anyone who likes _____ (a current pop group).

Categories should be mixed to include some 'fun' items.

Questionnaire

Pupils are given the strengths and weaknesses questionnaire (Figure 14.3) and a pencil and asked to complete it as honestly as possible. (These can be collected in later to give the teacher some idea of how the pupils view themselves.) Once this is done, the teacher tells them that they can have a short time to discuss their responses with someone they trust, to see if that person agrees with what they have written.

Middle phase – Open forum

The teacher facilitates a sensitive discussion using some of the following questions. A round can be used any time everyone's opinion is sought. Some sentence stems for rounds have been included.

Questions for discussion

- **Are you always aware of and appreciative of your own strengths?**
- **Do people see other people's strengths as more worthwhile than their own?**
- **Why should this be so?**
- **Are certain strengths generally held to be better than others?**
- **What strengths do you consider most desirable?**

Name:		Tutor group:		
Put a tick in the column that describes how good/bad you are at each of the following	**Good**	**Quite good**	**Not very good**	**Bad**
Being reliable				
Being honest				
Being hardworking				
Being kind				
Standing up for yourself				
Feeling confident in front of others				
Helping others out				
Getting work done on time				
Doing work carefully				
Being easy to get on with				
Keeping calm				
Thinking of other people's feelings				
Considering others' points of view				
Sorting out disputes calmly				
Sticking at difficult or boring tasks				
Finding things of interest to do out of school				
Being able to lead others				
Volunteering to be helpful				
Getting involved in clubs or societies				
Making friends				
Achieving goals				
Coping with changes in your life				
Cooperating with others in group activities				

Figure 14.3 Strengths and weaknesses questionnaire

Rounds

'I really appreciate it when people . . .'

'I really admire . . .'

'I would prefer to be . . .'

- What would help people to appreciate other people's strengths, even if they don't particularly admire them personally?
- Do people always admit their weaknesses? If not, why not?
- How do people deal with weaknesses?
- Do you have any good ways of dealing with area of weaknesses?
- Does anyone have a particular area of weakness at the moment that they would like some help with?

Use the scripts:

'Would it help if you . . .?'

'Would it help if I . . .?'

'Would it help if we . . .?'

Celebration

Encourage pupils to notice one another's strengths and acknowledge them by saying 'thank you' to the individual concerned.

Ending activity

Around the circle, each pupil in turn completes the sentence, 'One thing I really like about myself is . . .'. (No other pupils are allowed to make derogatory or negative comments about any individual's statement.)

Session 4   I am unique

Warm-up activity

Play things in common (see p. 108).

Develop game further

The teacher explains that he will call out different categories. Anyone in the named category enters the circle and greets others in that category. Pupils must try and remember who is in the same categories as themselves.

Examples of categories

- Anyone with a November birthday.
- Anyone who likes maths.
- Anyone who swims for a hobby.
- Anyone with a full set of grandparents.
- Anyone with size six feet.

Middle phase – Open forum

The teacher asks if any pupils were in all the same categories. If so, get them to sit in those groups and find ways in which they are different. Report back the differences.
   Teacher facilitates a discussion using the following questions:

- What sort of things do people have in common? e.g. physical needs, eating, sleeping etc; shared beliefs; interests; aims; likes/dislikes; similar backgrounds.
- What makes people different? e.g. appearance; beliefs; likes/dislikes; different backgrounds; interests etc.
- In a democracy everyone is supposed to be equal.

In pairs

Discuss what makes people think they or others are better? e.g. looks, wealth, intelligence, choice of clothes, interests, beliefs, family background etc.

Report back to whole group

Why do people face judgements on these values? e.g. Media influence, family influence, peer pressure, culture influence etc.

Round

'I don't feel equal when . . .'.

Get the group to summarise the ways in which they feel less than equal.

Open discussion

If an area of inequality emerges as common to the group, use the script 'Would it help if . . .?' to see if the class members can help one another with strategies for treating all individuals with respect.

Group cooperation

Play 'Points of contact' for a sense of group cooperation.

Celebration

Is there anyone in your class group who is always supportive and cooperative; someone who works well in a group?

Ending activity

Each pupil in turn states his/her name and makes one, two or three positive statements about him/herself (depending on the time and the level of openness and self-acceptance in the group), e.g. I am Thomas Turley. I am good at computer games, I am always on time. I share my possessions with other people.

No one can make derogatory remarks about another's statements. If any pupil has difficulty in finding three positive statements the other pupils can offer some on his/her behalf, e.g. 'Ahmed, you always work hard.' 'Sally, you are very considerate of others.' 'Gins, you are good fun.'

Session 5   Confidence

Materials

- **paper**
- **pencils**
- **container**

Warm-up activity

A pupil leaves the room. During his/her absence the others choose a person. The absent pupil returns and by questioning the participants has to guess the identity of the chosen person. Only 'yes', 'no' or 'don't know' answers can be given. Once the identity has been correctly guessed (perhaps players can be limited to three guesses) the process is repeated with new players.

Confidence

Pupils are given a piece of paper and pencil and asked to write down one thing that they lack confidence about or in doing, e.g. entering a room full of strangers, speaking out loud in class, personal appearance, going on a journey alone etc. The papers are folded and placed in a container.

The teacher facilitates an open discussion about the sorts of things that make people lack confidence e.g. criticism, being laughed at, failure, negative self-belief, being physically nervous, a new challenge.

What sort of things could help people become more confident? For example, praise, encouragement, practice, positive self-belief, experience etc.

Middle phase – Open forum

The teacher takes the pieces of paper out of the container, one at a time and reads out each statement. Every time this is done, pupils offer ideas and suggestions on how confidence could be gained in each area named using the script 'Would it help if they . . .?' (No one is allowed to try and name the author of any statement.)

The teacher asks the pupils to take one area of low confidence and write out an action plan at home, enlisting the help of others if necessary. Pupils are encouraged to put their action plans into practice.

Ending activity: creative visualisation

Visualisation

Pupils can sit or lie with eyes closed. The teacher explains that s/he is going to talk them through an epic struggle, which they must try and visualise in their mind's eye. One word of warning: a group of secondary pupils need to be confident enough to relax before they will enter into the process of creating a visualisation. Sometimes it is better to leave this activity until the group is well established with a greater degree of trust and cooperation than is present in a newly formed group.

You are standing at the bottom of a steep and rugged mountain which you have to climb. You look up, the peak is obscured by cloud. The rock face seems to go on forever. You feel daunted by the prospect of such a huge effort. Think of this feeling. It's the feeling you get when you have to do something really hard, that you don't want to do. Imagine now this feeling. Where is it? In the pit of your stomach? In your shoulders? Imagine it really strongly – weighing you down, holding you back . . .

You have to make a start. You adjust your backpack, take a deep breath and walk forward.

There is a path to start with. It's not too steep and you can walk fairly comfortably. Imagine a regular rhythm as you stride along. Picture yourself in motion one, two, one, two . . . the path becomes narrower and scattered rocks litter its surface. Dusty, hard-baked mud. Notice the rocks strewn along it. Imagine avoiding them by stepping over or walking around them. Perhaps you stumble sometimes as you carefully pick your way along the path. You are not walking with a regular rhythm now, but slowly and carefully . . . the path takes a steep upward turn. You begin to feel the effort of the ascent. The backpack feels really heavy, feel the weight of it on your back, the straps biting into your shoulders. Feel it pulling you down, draining your energy. Your leg muscles begin to ache, feel the pain in your calves and thighs – it's getting more and more intense . . .

You feel totally exhausted. Imagine this feeling very strongly. You have to rest. You stop, take off the backpack and sit down. Imagine the relief as you stop climbing. Feel the weight of your limbs, heavy and relaxed. Think of the good feeling of removing the backpack. You sit and rest, eat food and drink. Perhaps you doze a little . . .

You have to go on, but are reluctant to make a start. Imagine urging yourself to get up and go on. You don't want that heavy backpack on again, but you know you have to. Nag yourself, encourage yourself – you have to continue . . .

At last you are ready to move on. The path continues to climb steeply and now it is entering the clouds. You feel the damp chill falling slowly around you, enveloping you in its clammy, cold grip. It's so cold now, you can feel it right in your bones. Think of its penetrating coldness, imagine how you are feeling . . .

On you trudge in your silent, grey, misty world. You feel very alone, the silence is overwhelming. Think of how alone you are in your chilly grey world. Feel the loneliness of your situation . . .

Gradually, you emerge from the cloud layer. The sun warms your face. Feel its deep, penetrating rays bringing life back to your frozen limbs. At last you can see the summit, but the path has run out. You prepare yourself mentally for the final effort . . .

You now have to climb, inch by inch. You look for hand and foot holds and pull yourself slowly up. You feel nervous about slipping. Each movement is slow and careful. Your arms and legs ache from the effort. You are totally exhausted. You grit your teeth with determination and haul yourself upward. Feel the effort and determination in every inch of your body. See the summit coming gradually closer. You know you can do it . . .

At last, the final pull and you are there. Imagine the excitement, the feeling of success and achievement – you have done it. You have conquered the mountain, your fear, your exhaustion and won. Enjoy the exhilaration of your success. You feel happy and contented.

Session 6   Friendship

Materials

- flipchart
- pen
- blackboard
- chalk
- paper
- coloured pens/paints

Warm-up activity

One pupil begins a sentence, e.g. 'I went to the zoo and saw an elephant'; the second pupil repeats and adds another animal: 'I went to the zoo and saw an elephant and a tiger.' This continues around the circle with each pupil repeating the previous sentence and adding another animal until someone makes a mistake or cannot think of a new animal. That person begins a new sentence.

Examples

I went to the shop and bought _____

In my lunchbox I had _____

I swam under the sea and saw _____

I went to the dog's home for a _____

Friendship brainstorm

Ask pupils to brainstorm all the attributes of friendship – e.g. kindness, cooperation, shared interests, loyalty, trust, generosity, caring, sharing, support and write them on a flipchart or blackboard.

Middle phase – Open Forum

The teacher facilitates a discussion using the following questions.

- **Why do people like to have friends?**
- **Does everyone need friends?**
- **Are all friendships good?**
- **If not, when can a friendship be harmful (e.g. bad influences, domination, sycophantic relationships)?**
- **Do different people look for different things in friends?**
- **Can people be 'friendly' to everyone, even if they're not real friends?**

Round

'I am a good friend when I . . .'.

The pupils can make a poster, advertising themselves as a friend. They must include all the qualities that they possess, and which they think would make them attractive.

Celebration

Pupils recall times when they noticed someone being a good friend to someone else, not to themselves. They thank the person for being a good friend.

Ending activity

Pupils form pairs with someone who is not a close friend. Each member of the pair in turn has a minute to tell the other as much about him/herself as possible, e.g. likes/dislikes, hobbies, beliefs, favourite programmes etc. The pair then take turns to relate back to each other as much as they can remember of what they've been told.

Close with a round when each person introduces their partner by name with one positive piece of information about him/her, i.e. 'This is . . . he/she . . .'.

Session 7   Loneliness

Materials

- flipchart
- pen or chalkboard
- chalk
- pencils
- paper
- container

Warm-up activity

Word association around the circle with two claps in between each item, e.g. 'book' clap, clap; 'page' clap, clap; 'letters' clap, clap; 'parcels' clap, clap; 'birthdays' clap, clap.

If anyone falters or cannot think of a word, they begin a new sequence. See how fast the participants can get this going.

Loneliness

The teacher tells the pupils that everyone experiences lonely times. S/he asks them to brainstorm occasions when they felt lonely and writes them down on paper or board.

Examples

When I split up with my best friend.

When I had to stay with my Aunt and Uncle.

When I travelled to London on the train on my own.

Middle phase – Open forum

The teacher facilitates a sensitive discussion about loneliness, using the following questions:

- **What does it feel like to be lonely (e.g. nervous, frightened, uncared-for, depressed, miserable, and resentful)?**
- **What can happen to people in extreme loneliness (e.g. severe depression, physical and mental disorders and, sometimes, suicide)?**
- **What type of people might be particularly susceptible to loneliness (e.g. old people living alone, people living in a foreign country, disabled people)?**
- **Do you think enough is done to help lonely people?**
- **Do you ever consciously think about helping people who are lonely?**

Paired exercise

In your pair think of times when people may feel lonely at school. Write an example on a piece of paper and put it in a container.

The teacher reads from one piece of paper at a time. No situation is attributed to a pair and the class makes suggestions on ways of dealing with it. Pupils make suggestions using the script 'Would it help if they . . .?', 'Would it help if I . . .?', 'Would it help if we . . .?'.

Any ideas that might result in changes in school policy or procedure should be noted and taken to the school council or relevant member of the senior management team.

Ending activity

One player leaves the room. The remaining players think of a rule which will govern the way they respond, e.g. person who is talking must cross legs (others must not). Or the replies must contain a specific word, e.g. 'actually'. Or they must touch their right ear while replying etc. The absent player returns and questions the class in turn about any topic, e.g. the weather, pets, breakfasts – and by observing their replies the player must guess the rule which governs their responses. When he has done this a new player leaves the room and a different rule is agreed on. It might be a good idea to set a time limit in which the rule has to be guessed.

Session 8   Being popular

Materials

- photocopied sheets of pupils' names
- pencils

Warm-up activity

Play waves

This is played by having a circle of seats equal in number to the class members. One person volunteers to be in the middle. (Make sure they are of a robust temperament and not vulnerable to exclusion by the social group.) The whole class then moves round from one seat to the next in a continuous wave of motion and the person in the centre tries to sit on the vacant chair. Once the group gets the knack of this, it is extremely hard to get in to the chair because it is not ever really left vacant.

Ask the person in the middle what it felt like to be left out. When the person sits down again, ask the whole group to say what they feel when they are left out. 'I feel . . . What did it feel like to be part of the main group?'

Being popular

On the back of their photocopied sheets, the pupils are asked to write down what they consider to be the five most important details that makes a person popular, e.g. good looks, being trendy, having money, being good at sports, being cheerful, being kind etc. One pupil can read out his list and the others raise their hands if they also wrote that attribute on their list. This can be done several times to establish what the participants consider to be the most important attributes of being popular.

Middle phase – Open forum

The teacher facilitates a discussion on being popular by asking the following questions. How important a consideration is 'being popular' in your life? What do you do in order to increase your popularity?

In pairs

Talk about an occasion when you did something to make yourself more popular which afterwards you wished you hadn't done.

Whole-group discussion

What do they see as the advantages to being popular? Is there ever a time when people look as if they are popular but it is not a true picture? For example, befriending people who are rich or famous.

Do they think that being popular has any disadvantages? For example unwelcome attention, having to maintain an 'image', having to be a leader, others being jealous and resentful. What can this class do to ensure that everyone is included and people do not feel left out?

Use the script:

'Would it help if we . . .'

Celebration

Is there anyone in this group that you would like to thank because they are good at making everyone feel included?

Ending activity

Pupils vote on who they consider to be the five most popular people in the country. Anyone can propose a name and the others vote by raising their hands. The teacher or a pupil can write down the names and scores to discover the 'top 5'.

Session 9   How to listen well

Warm-up activity

Pupils form pairs. Teacher tells them that each pair is going to converse about a holiday they enjoyed. They can question each other about aspects of the holiday and compare experiences. The teacher gives the rules for conversing and after each minute s/he explains the new rule, which can be one of the following:

- back to back;
- facing each other but with eyes closed;
- facing each other but looking somewhere else;
- in mime;
- in gobble-de-gook (i.e. nonsense words);
- standing stiffly to attention;
- lying relaxed on the floor facing each other;
- deliberately thinking about something else while they are listening to partner.

Middle phase – Open forum

The teacher asks pupils:

- what helped them to listen well, e.g. eye contact, relaxed posture, concentrating, understanding language?
- what hindered them from listening, e.g. not concentrating, not maintaining eye contact, not understanding language?
- what other things might affect their ability to listen well in lessons; boredom, not understanding subject, feeling emotional, tiredness, feeling unwell?
- why is it an advantage to be able to listen well?

Encourage the pupils to think all round this subject, not just in the school context. Clarify the skills needed for good listening, e.g.

- relaxed posture;
- maintaining eye contact;
- clarifying what has been said by questioning or repeating the main gist;
- maintaining concentration.

Celebration

Is there anyone in your class that you would like to thank because they are a good listener?

Ending activity

Putting these listening skills into practice, each member of the pair talks to the other for two minutes about their families. When both have done this, they take it in turns to report back to the other as much as they can remember of what they were told.

Session 10   Name calling

Warm-up activity

- Play 'Who are you?' (p. 110)
- The teacher follows this by calling out different categories; anyone in the named category must change seats.

Examples

Anyone whose name begins with the letter S.	Anyone whose name consists of six letters.
Anyone with an 'A' in their name.	Anyone whose name ends with N.

Middle phase – Open forum

The teacher begins a discussion about having fun with their names, but sometimes people call each other names which are unkind. What things are unkind comments often made about?

Examples

- **appearance;**
- **the way they talk.**

How do you feel when you are called unkind names? Begin with an open discussion and if there is plenty of response have a round: 'When someone calls me an unkind name, I feel . . .'.

The teacher asks for suggestions of ways in which nasty name-calling could be stopped.

Use the script

'Would it help if . . .?' And remember *no names negatively*.

Open forum could include role play of situations when name calling becomes unkind. Pupils can explore ways of dealing assertively with unkind words.

Celebration

Is there anyone you want to thank because they can speak assertively without becoming aggressive or personal?

Ending activity

Action name game

Pupils stand in a circle. Each person in turn says his/her name prefixed by an alliterative verb.

Examples

I am jumping Jake.   I am tunnelling Tom.   I am motoring Meg.

These actions can be accompanied by a mime which the other circle members copy.

15 Games and activities for Circle Time

In this chapter games and activities are catalogued alphabetically. Each entry includes the basic game, the materials needed and a description of what to do, followed by ways in which it could be extended or varied. You might find it simpler to play the initial game first, then once you are confident with the way that it goes, you can begin to branch out and extend it. All games have great potential to make people feel good and equal potential to destroy morale. For instance, the game 'You're positive' (p. 111), can greatly enhance the self-esteem of the person who is asked to leave the room if the comments are truly positive. On the other hand, the class could use a game like this one to 'wind up' the teacher by only saying negative things. You will have to develop an atmosphere of trust in the group by using 'safe' games such as 'Keeper of the keys', then move on to more 'risky' ones. You will quickly acquire a sense of when a game is going well, or when it is 'unsafe'. If you think the group is not yet ready for any activity, drop it and do something that you know will go well.

When playing games, you also need to give yourself permission to fail. Tell the class that you are learning about these games too and you don't know if they will work or not. You can encourage the group to evaluate the games and they can suggest ways of improving or developing them. Once you have more confidence, you will become very skilled at drawing out the rules, skills and learning points that emerge from your particular group in relation to a game. Any learning point that emerges can also be explored using drama and role-play techniques in pairs, in small groups or involving the whole group. The synopsis at the beginning of the games and activities (Figure 15.1) shows the main purpose of each one, but here again, you will find your own purposes emerging as you explore each game and may well feel that you want to rewrite the index at the end!

	Cooperation	Concentration	Imagination	Listening	Speaking	Observation	Creativity	Thinking	Self-affirmation	Self-esteem	Assertiveness	Appreciation	Laughter/fun	Empathy	Self-disclosure	Confidence
A star for a second		•											•			
A worry shared		•									•		•		•	•
And another thing	•					•							•			
Believe me?				•	•			•					•	•		
Chinese mimes	•					•							•			
Copy me, or 'Simon says'	•	•		•						•			•			•
Dealing with failure				•	•			•		•			•			•
Double Dutch	•		•			•		•								
Electric squeeze	•	•											•			
Gender difference?								•				•	•			
Gender 2								•				•	•			
Gloop	•					•							•			
Good try	•	•	•					•		•			•			
Gotcha									•					•	•	•
Guess the phrase	•	•				•							•			
Guided walk	•							•								
I am a chair!									•	•					•	•
Identification cards	•									•			•			
Keeper of the keys		•		•				•		•						•
Life line										•						
Man's best friend		•				•	•	•								
Moan on	•	•				•				•						•
My gang		•				•				•						
My other half	•												•			
My tribe name		•	•							•						•
Negotiating			•	•	•				•		•			•		•
Newspaper stories		•							•		•		•			
Number call		•		•									•	•		
Opting out			•							•			•	•		
Parental concerns				•				•					•			•
Pass the action		•				•				•		•	•		•	
Pass the snake						•		•		•			•		•	
Play the game		•	•	•	•	•		•					•			
Positive news		•			•	•				•			•			
Problem-solving	•		•	•				•		•			•			
Red Queen	•					•							•		•	•
Reflections	•					•		•		•			•	•		
Ring on a string									•	•			•		•	
Saying sorry			•	•							•		•	•	•	•
Setbacks	•	•		•									•			•
Similarities and differences		•								•			•			•
Tease			•								•	•	•			
Things in common					•				•	•	•		•			•
Touchdown								•		•	•		•			
Who are you?			•					•	•				•			•
You're positive			•		•								•			•
Zoom – Eek									•	•		•	•	•		

Figure 15.1 Key to games and activities for Circle Time

A star for a second

What to do

Each participant chooses a celebrity who they would like to be and writes the name on a piece of paper. They also write what they think they have in common with this person and/or why they would like to be this particular star. The teacher collects all the names and, one at a time, reads out the celebrity named. Participants have to guess who chose each celebrity; they are allowed one guess each. NB Make sure that there are no negative put-downs in this activity.

How this could be varied and developed

Participants can discuss what they admire about the celebrity they chose. Do they think celebrities are chosen for the right or wrong reasons? Do they think some celebrities are paid too much, e.g. film stars, football players?

A worry shared

What to do

Participants sit in an inward-facing circle. They are each given a piece of paper and anonymously write one worry that they have in the class or group.

Examples
- speaking in front of others;
- being laughed at;
- arriving late;
- feeling isolated;
- being asked questions/put on the spot.

The pieces of paper are folded and placed in a container and participants are invited to each take one and in turn, read out the 'worry'. They are instructed that they may say 'Yes' to any worry they also experience, but they are not allowed to negate any, even if they do not share it. NB Discourage participants from trying to guess who wrote a particular worry.

How this could be varied or developed

1. The teacher can facilitate a discussion on worries and have a round of 'I feel worried when . . .'. In the circle, participants can discuss strategies they have developed for dealing with worries.
2. Individuals can be given the opportunity to ask for help with a particular worry. The teacher could say 'Does anyone need help with any particular worry that they have?' The group can then offer help, advice and support using the script 'Would it help if I?', 'Would it help if you?' As in all Open Forum discussions, the person who asked for help may accept or reject the advice.

And another thing

What to do

Participants stand in an inward-facing circle. In silence one person makes a simple sound. The next person copies the sound and adds another, the next copies the two previous sounds and adds a third and so on around the circle until a player forgets the sequence or gets a sound wrong. Once the sequence is broken, a new one begins, but this time, instead of a sound s/he initiates a movement.

Make sure that a player doesn't get too bogged down in trying to remember the sequence. If someone is having real difficulties start the game again. If you know someone is likely to find this game very hard, s/he can be the one to start or can be near the beginning.

How this can be varied or developed

1. This game can be played as a verbal memory game instead of a visual one, e.g. 'I went on holiday and packed . . .' or 'My grandmother went to market and bought . . .'.
2. In the circle participants can discuss the issue of memory. They consider whether they think they have good/bad memories. What memories stay 'bright' – which ones thankfully get lost?
3. The teacher can lead a discussion on types of memory, visual/auditory/kinesthetic and encourage pupils to identify their preferred learning style.
4. Do they think they can improve their memory?
5. Individuals can ask for help with certain aspects of memory and learn from the strategies other members of the group use to remember things.

Believe me?

What to do

Participants are given a prepared list of value statements with true and false columns in which they tick their responses.

Examples
- A doctor is a better person than a refuse collector.
- People should be judged by the clothes they wear.
- Young people should always respect adults.
- Rich people are nicer than poor people.
- People with learning disabilities are stupid.
- People who get high grades are better than people who get low grades.
- Old people are a nuisance.

How this can be varied or developed

1. In pairs then small groups, participants compare their responses.
2. In the circle discuss what sort of value judgements people make about others, e.g. appearance, clothes, social standing, age, able-bodied, intellect.
3. Can the group come up with a set of values to admire and promote that would allow equal opportunities?

Chinese mimes

What to do

Participants are divided into groups of six or eight. Each group forms a small circle and a member of each group thinks of a short, but fairly complicated task to mime. Participants must not practice or talk about their mimes.

All other participants except for the player next to the one with the mime close their eyes. The performer shows his/her mime to the next player who then taps the third player, who opens his/her eyes. The second player then repeats the mime, and so on until the mime has been passed right round the circle. Each player says what s/he thinks the task was and the originator tells the group what it actually was. The next person then thinks of a task to mime and the game continues until all the participants have had a turn at miming a task.

Encourage participants to make their actions clear and to avoid deliberately changing them.

How this could be varied or developed

1. In a circle, the group members can discuss how events can be altered or distorted in the telling. How can this lead to problems in life? For example, tales can be very different from the truth by the time they reach the fourth or fifth person.
2. Develop the idea of distorted communication. Individuals can say how they feel when they are misrepresented by distortion of the truth and share strategies for dealing with such incidents. There is great scope for role-play to show ways in which information is distorted and the hurt/misunderstandings/chaos that can ensue.

Copy me – or 'Simon Says'!

What to do

Any group member can be designated as the leader. The leader initiates an action accompanied by the words 'I say' or 'Simon says', e.g. 'I say touch your toes.' If the instruction is preceded by 'I say' then the class copies it. If the action is not preceded by 'I say' the class ignores it. There is plenty of opportunity to 'catch people out' with this game and so look at the issues around making mistakes, how we feel when we make mistakes and the value of mistakes in the learning process. There is also opportunity to discuss the need to keep the learning environment 'safe' by avoiding ridicule and 'put-downs'.

How it could be varied

1. The leader can start an action which the group copies. When the leader changes the action, the whole group follows suit. Then one person is chosen as a detective. They go outside the room while a leader is chosen. On return, they stand in the middle of the circle and have to work out which group member is changing the action. The detective has to keep turning in the middle, they cannot stand still and stare at one person. They have to keep 'whipping' around to test their theory out.
2. The action can be playing a musical instrument as the leader of an orchestra. The whole group has to play the same instrument. When the detective returns to the room, s/he has to find the leader of the orchestra.

Dealing with failure

What to do
Divide the group into pairs. In turn, each participant chooses an area of failure which s/he relates to his/her partner. The partner must think of and say as many genuine positive responses as can be made. The initial participant isn't allowed to respond with 'yes ... but ...'. S/he has to say 'That's one way of looking at it ...'.

Give examples of failure
- low grade in a piece of work;
- failure to get girl/boyfriend of one's choice;
- being left out of a sport's team;
- being excluded from a social event;
- unable to understand in a teaching situation;
- job application turned down.

How this can be varied or developed
1. In the circle discuss how failure makes you feel. Have a round 'When I fail at something I feel ...'.
2. Brainstorm why failure is worse for some people than for others.
3. Brainstorm effective strategies for dealing with failure.
4. Discuss any ways in which failure can be seen in a positive light.
5. Look at example of where you can apply negative or positive thinking – e.g. my glass is half empty/full!

Double Dutch

(It would probably be better to do this activity after an initial warm-up round or game so that people are feeling more relaxed and less self-conscious.)

What to do
The group is divided into pairs and each pair is given a pre-written card with a situation to initiate dialogue. (See next page for situations.) The pairs can only talk gibberish. They must try to convey meaning through tone of voice, inflection, facial expressions and gestures. They need to imagine what they are saying before they 'speak'.

How this could be varied or developed
1. Whole group discussion on importance of body language.
2. Participants can discuss in their pairs how clearly they were able to convey their meaning to each other and how often they were misinterpreted or not understood at all. The paired work could be followed by a group discussion or round about being understood/misunderstood.
3. Repeat the exercise in groups of four with group situations (see next page).
4. In pairs, the participants could carry on a 'conversation' using drawings and symbols only (no written words).
5. Participants could discuss the importance of language and how someone with language problems might be affected.

Situations for pairs

- Person asks for directions to football ground.
- Person seeks shop assistant's help in choosing a Fathers' Day present.
- Person teaches pupil how to make a cake.
- Person wants to find out all the details of a package holiday from a travel agent.
- Employer speaks to worker who has not completed a task satisfactorily.
- Customer in restaurant talks to waiter about menu and orders meal.
- Two people discuss and prepare a picnic meal.
- Person tells friend about dog training classes s/he has been attending.
- Person complains to shop assistant about shoddy goods.
- Patient seeks doctor's advice over ailment.

Situations for groups

- People are in a lift which breaks down.
- Policeman interviews witnesses to an accident.
- Leader discusses organizing a party with team members.
- Group discusses a chosen television programme.
- Group discusses merits/disadvantages of living in the town or country.
- Group talk about how to entertain a foreign visitor.

Electric squeeze

What to do

The group members all hold hands in the circle. One person starts off by squeezing the hand next door. The squeeze gets passed round the circle. It can be sent in both directions at once and variations can include double squeezes that change the direction of 'flow'. A one-minute timer can be used to ensure that the 'squeeze' returns to the beginning of the circle and a small group of students do not dominate the game.

Gender difference?

What to do

You will need two large sheets of card and pens. The teacher has two large sheets of card divided in half vertically. The participants are asked to get into two groups, one boys and the other girls. In the groups, brainstorm the similarities and differences between males and females. The group writes the brainstorm ideas on the card. Participants are encouraged to think of real considerations and not make facetious or ill-considered remarks. Once this activity has been done in single gender groups, the two lists are compared in the whole group and the teacher can lead a discussion as to whether there are real differences between the genders. If so, what might cause these?

How this can be developed

1. The teacher leads a discussion on the process of working in single gender then mixed gender groups. Are mixed groups as successful as single gender groups? What are the advantages and disadvantages of each?
2. Can the genders really understand each other or do they 'think' in different ways?
3. Are male/female priorities different?

Gender 2

What to do

You will need dry-marker or chalkboard or card and pens. The teacher has two large sheets of card or the board divided in half vertically. Group members are asked to brainstorm all the things they believe girls/boys are better at. Participants are encouraged to give thoughtful, well-considered responses.

How this can be developed

1. The group can discuss whether they consider boys/girls really have greater aptitudes/ abilities in certain areas and why this should be so, e.g. biological functioning, sociological considerations etc.
2. Should boys/girls have equal opportunities in all areas?
3. Does the school have an equal opportunities policy? If so, how does it affect different members of the school community?

Gloop

What to do

Some imaginary slime is 'thrown' from one group member to another. The 'slime' always lands on the person's face and as it is pulled off, the group makes sucking, slurping noises. The game generates good eye contact and much laughter. It gives power to people who rarely have any and it can be a good energiser if the mood in the group is rather 'flat'.

Good try!

What to do

The group sit in an inward-facing circle with one person standing in the centre. The person in the middle has an object such as a ruler which s/he uses to mime a common activity such as brushing teeth, combing hair, spreading butter etc. Group members have to guess the activity. If a person gets it right, the one in the middle says 'Well done' and gives the object to the new person who thinks of a mime. If they get it wrong, the one in the middle says 'Good try' and carries on miming until someone makes a correct guess.

How this could be varied or developed

1. Group members can mime their particular hobby and the others have to guess what the hobby is. Everyone who has the same hobby then changes places.
2. In the circle discuss what it feels like to be congratulated on getting something right.
3. How does it feel to get it wrong, but be told 'Good try' rather than 'You're wrong'?
4. Discuss the power of the way we say things to each other and brainstorm helpful and unhelpful ways of pointing out mistakes. This can lead on to role-play of helpful ways of giving and receiving feedback.

Gotcha

What to do

Participants sit in an inward-facing circle. The teacher spins an empty bottle in the centre. Whenever the bottle stops spinning, the participant sitting opposite the bottleneck speaks on a chosen topic. The person who has just spoken then spins the bottle to identify the next person.

Topics for self-disclosure
- What I like about myself.
- What I dislike about myself.
- Something I worry about.
- Something I would like to achieve etc.

How this could be varied and developed

1. Any topic can be chosen for Gotcha. It becomes a more amusing and fun way of having a round and eliciting views or opinions on the topic to be discussed.
2. Gotcha can lead on into an open-forum discussion on the chosen topic, e.g. it can be used for Records of Achievement or goal-setting in Personal Development Plans. Individuals who want help in achieving goals or overcoming fears etc. can ask for advice and support from their peers.

Guess the phrase

What to do
The teacher will need two prepared sheets of well-known phrases/proverbs (one person has sheet A and the other sheet B). The participants work in pairs with a list each. One person has to draw a picture to illustrate the proverb/phrase and the other tries to guess the phrase or proverb for each illustration. They are awarded one point for each correct answer.

How it can be varied or developed
1. Participants form two teams and work out a set of mimed phrases/proverbs for the other team to guess.
2. In small groups participants could create a short scene which illustrates a phrase. Each group in turn can act out their scene and then ask the other participants to guess the phrase.
3. Participants could write or draw (cartoon style) a story illustrating a phrase or proverb.
4. In the circle, have a discussion about the purpose of these kinds of phrases and proverbs. Each person could state one that has meaning for them and give the reason why.

Lists for Guess the phrase

List A
1. Time flies.
2. Don't count your chickens before they've hatched.
3. Too good to be true.
4. Too many cooks spoil the broth.
5. Don't cry over spilt milk.
6. Every cloud has a silver lining.
7. Look before you leap.
8. Two wrongs don't make a right.
9. A fool and his money are soon parted.
10. Happy as a pig in clover.
11. Blood is thicker than water.
12. A drowning man will clutch at a straw.
13. All that glitters is not gold.
14. A watched pot never boils.
15. Cold hands, warm heart.

List B
1. Curiosity killed the cat.
2. Don't put all your eggs in one basket.
3. Don't throw the baby out with the bath water.
4. Empty vessels make the most sound.
5. The early bird catches the worm.
6. Great oaks from little acorns grow.
7. It's a small world.
8. Laughter is the best medicine.
9. Let sleeping dogs lie.
10. Like father, like son.
11. Make hay while the sun shines.
12. One man's meat is another man's poison.
13. The best things come in small packages.
14. There's no smoke without fire.
15. The way to a man's heart is through his stomach.

Guided walk

What to do

Participants work in pairs. The whole group sets up a short obstacle course with chairs, bags, books, bins, desks etc. (Several obstacle courses can be used at once, or one for the whole group, depending on the availability of space.) One of the pair is blindfolded and led through the obstacle course by his/her partner's verbal instructions. They then reverse roles. The obstacle course is rearranged at the end of each turn. If the group is very boisterous, just let one pair work at a time with the whole class watching. Each pair has to aim to 'get through with no bumps'.

How this can be varied or developed

1. In the circle, discuss times when we need to trust one another. What makes it easy/difficult to trust people? The group could have a round of 'I find it hard to trust people when . . .' or 'I find it easy to trust people when . . .'.
2. In the circle, participants can discuss how it felt to be 'blind' and what it might be like for someone who is visually impaired or blind.
3. How might loss of sight affect the individual and how might it affect others around him/her?
4. When the sense of sight is missing, which other senses are used to compensate?

I am a chair!

What to do

The teacher supplies a collection of everyday objects such as a coat, vase, pen, curtain, bucket, plate etc. to stimulate imagination. Each participant is given an object to think about. You can start with objects in the room, then branch out into objects that pupils imagine. They are to look for all the positive features of their chosen or assigned object. A round follows in which each person names his/her object (in the first person) and expands on all its qualities. They are asked to be as imaginative and inventive as possible.

Example

I am a chair. I am strong and durable. I am attractive to look at because I am beautifully carved and my seat is covered in soft strong leather. I provide people with somewhere to rest or work. I enhance a room with my appearance. NB Start with a confident person so that the shy and embarrassed have time to get used to the activity.

How it could be varied or developed

- **Pupils are asked which object they would choose to represent themselves and why. Have a round 'If I were an animal, I'd be a . . . because . . .'.**

Identification cards

What to do

Each participant is given a piece of card and told to make it into his/her personal identification card. They are asked to include details of themselves on the card which shows their uniqueness (rather than general descriptions that might apply to many others). Ensure you guide them to only write the positive aspects.

Examples
- **They can write their name.**
- **Attach a photograph.**
- **Make a thumb print.**
- **Detail any unique physical feature that they value.**
- **Detail positive aspects of personality.**
- **Give any special ideas only they have.**
- **Any special achievement.**

NB Be ready to help out any individuals who do not see themselves as unique and valuable.

How this could be varied and developed

- **In the circle discuss in what ways individuals are unique and the importance/value of each individual.**

This activity can be extended to examine how I feel about how I see myself. How I feel about how others see me. What I would need to change in order for others to see me differently.

Keeper of the keys

This is a game of stealth. The group can construct the story that accompanies the game, but the essential ingredients are a chair in the middle of the circle with a pupil sat on it blindfolded and under the chair, a large bunch of keys. The idea is that the keys represent some treasure or something of value, which has been stolen and is being guarded by the pupil on the chair. One at a time, other pupils in the group are chosen to attempt to recapture the treasure. They have to be as quiet as possible and if the pupil on the chair

94

hears any sound, s/he shouts 'stop' and points in the direction of the sound. If the challenge is correct, the discovered pupil has to sit on the floor and become an obstacle to the next pupil who attempts to recapture the treasure. Once someone succeeds in picking up the keys without being detected, they can become the new Keeper of the keys.

How this can be varied or developed

1. The teacher asks the group 'If the treasure was a target, what would you like to achieve at school?' Many members of the group might suggest targets of various kinds; academic, sporting, social etc. These can be written down and pupils encouraged to identify with one or more of them.
2. One of these targets can be chosen and the whole group can examine the question, 'What are the obstacles that stop us from achieving this target?'
3. The question, 'Does anyone want help with a specific target?' can be asked and then the group is given the opportunity to help an individual using the script 'Would it help if you . . .'. An action plan could be written from this activity and given to the individual.

Life line

What to do

Participants will need large sheets of paper and pencils. Each person is given a sheet of paper and asked to draw a line. The line represents their life so far. On one side of the line they write all the positive things that have happened in their life and on the other side all the negative things.

Example					
Positive	Learned to swim	Played Mary in Nativity	Went to Portugal	New class teacher	Had photo in paper
Age	5	6	7	8	9 etc.
Negative	Broke front tooth	Grandpa died	Didn't like teacher Broke arm	Broke up with best friend	

How this could be varied or developed

1. In circle discuss whether life is an even mix of positive and negative things or more of one than the other.
2. What would you like to see on your lifeline in the future? Is there anything you can do to bring it about?
3. What do you hope will be the next major event on your lifeline? What do you have to do in order to be certain it will happen?
4. The lifeline can be drawn with peaks and troughs rather than on a straight line. This gives a pictorial representation of the 'highs' and 'lows' of life.

Man's best friend

What to do

Each participant writes his/her name on a piece of paper and puts it into a container. One at a time, the facilitator draws out a name from the container and invites a participant to choose a dog that would suit the named person.

The person whose name is on the slip of paper can reply by agreeing or making their own statement:

'Yes, I'd like a . . .' or

'No, I'd rather have a . . .'.

How this could be varied or developed

1. In the circle, participants can discuss what attributes they would look for in choosing a dog.
2. What would they like a dog for, e.g. companionship, protection, image, physical appearance etc.?
3. This can be extended to the attributes and qualities the group members would look for in a friend.
4. How would they have to change in order to be a better friend to other people? This can be followed by a round 'I am a good friend when . . .' or 'A good friend to me is someone who . . .'.

Moan on

What to do

The teacher asks the group members to brainstorm all the things in life that irritate them. These can be people, places, situations, TV programmes etc. (No comment must be made about any of the ideas, they are all noted down on a large sheet of paper.) Each member of the group then lists their ten greatest moans in order of magnitude with the biggest as number one.

How this can be varied or developed

1. In the circle have a round 'The biggest irritation in my life is . . .'.
2. Discuss why certain things annoy some people and not others.

3. In the light of the discussion, encourage pupils to evaluate how valid they now think their grumbles are. Has anyone changed their opinion? What made them change it?
4. A grumble/irritation that occurred often in the group could be discussed and an action plan produced on how to avoid, change or deal with this grumble. It may be helpful to role-play the irritation or grumble in order to clarify what exactly goes on. Doubling (as explained on page 88) can be used to discuss more helpful ways forward.

My gang

What to do
In turn pupils are chosen to stand in the centre of the circle and invite group members to join his/her gang by naming a category for entry.

Examples

> Anyone who likes *Casualty* can be in my gang.
>
> Anyone who plays roller hockey can be in my gang.
>
> Anyone why supports Manchester United can be in my gang.
>
> And so on.

Anyone who fits the category goes to stand by the speaker in the centre of the circle. A new gang leader is chosen and group members move on to a new 'gang' each time they fit in with the requirements of the category stated. Individuals keep a tally of the number of gangs they 'belonged' to. At the end pupils return to their seats in the circle. Those who belonged to one gang stand up and are applauded by the rest. Then those who belonged to two, then three up to the maximum number of 'gangs' in the game. Each time a group of pupils stand up they are applauded by the pupils sitting down. (Minority groups should then get the maximum applause!) NB It is important that participants do not base their choices of 'gang' on personalities but on categories.

How this can be varied or developed
1. In the circle participants can discuss the pros and cons of belonging to a 'gang'.
2. Do they normally belong to just one or several different groups and why?
3. Have a round of 'I feel . . . when I am left out.'
4. The activity can be followed by a round of 'I feel included when . . .'.

My other half

Why do this?
- to create random pairings;
- as a fun way to warm up the group.

What to do
You will need photocopies of symbols such as the ones in Figure 15.2. The symbols are cut in half and there must be enough for each group member to have one half of a

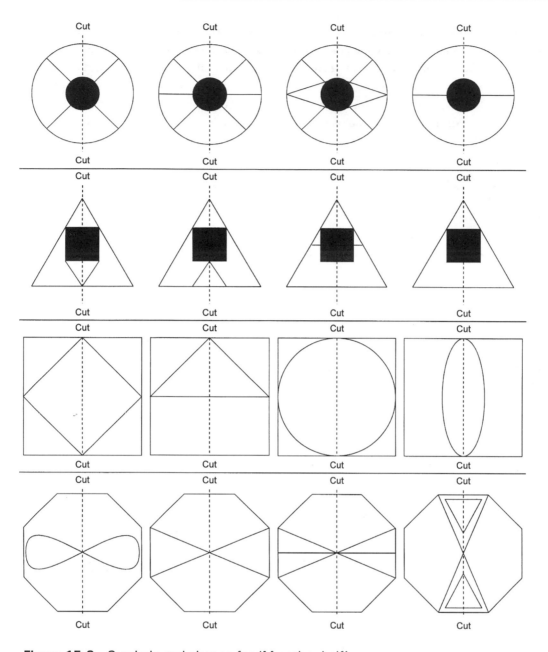

Figure 15.2 Symbols and shapes for 'My other half'

matched pair. The teacher explains that each participant will be given half a symbol. On the command 'Go', participants mingle and, without any verbal communication, they have a set time (2.5 minutes) to try and locate the person who is holding the matching half of their symbol. This person then becomes their partner. At the end of the set time, any participants without partners can receive help. Alternatively, they can take turns to 'draw' their symbol in the air until everyone is matched up.

How this could be varied

1. **This activity can be used as an ice-breaker for new groups. After the pairs are formed, they are given five minutes to find out as much about their partners as possible. The group then forms a circle and each participant introduces his/her partner to the group**

stating three facts about him/her, e.g. 'This is Joe Atkins. His favourite food is roast chicken. He plays rugby for a local team and he has a German Shepherd dog called Tyson.'

2. In an established group, the activity is a good way to create random pairs for further paired exercises if you want to give the participants the opportunity to work with people they would not necessarily choose as partners. One of the paired exercises on the next pages could then be used.

My tribe name

What to do

In groups of six upwards (depending on memory/concentration) each participant thinks of an Indian name and a mimed sign to represent the name.

Examples

Name	Sign
Running Water	Two fingers running followed by fingers of both hands 'rippling'
Sleeping Dog	Hands together by side of head, followed by first and second fingers of both hands making 'ears'

In turn, the participants say their names and perform their mimes. Other group members have to try to remember these names. The game continues with one player stating his/her name and performing the associated mime then saying another player's name and performing the relevant mime. This player then repeats his/her name and mime and addresses a third player with the appropriate name and mime. The game continues like this, but if a player gets a name/mime wrong s/he is out. Players can perform the mime only.

How this can be varied or developed

Participants can discuss what sort of descriptive names they would choose for themselves

Examples
- helpful, reliable, fun, sporty, out-going Bill,
- kind, caring, hard-working, fashionable Nina etc.

Negotiating

What to do

The teacher has a selection of situations in which two people disagree about something. Participants form pairs and role-play negotiating a compromise, which is acceptable to both of them. The teacher tells participants they must only agree to something they feel happy with.

Examples
- A wants to go to the cinema, and B wants to go swimming, but they both want the other's company.
- A wants chips for tea and B wants roast, but they can only prepare one meal.
- A wants to holiday abroad somewhere hot but B cannot tolerate the heat. They want to go somewhere together.
- A has a work deadline to complete for his/her boss B, but cannot finish the work by that time.
- A and B want to buy their father a joint present. A wants to buy something useful, e.g. a jumper but B wants to buy something just for pleasure, e.g. a large cake.

Check out
Encourage participants to try and play roles 'for real'.

How this could be varied and developed
1. The teacher can lead a discussion on how easy/difficult it is to listen to the other person when you want your own way.
2. Did one person just 'give in' and let the other have his/her own way?
3. Did either member of the partnership get angry and aggressive in order to get his/her own way?
4. What helped you to arrive at a compromise?
5. Can you think of any situations that require you to be able to negotiate successfully?
6. Role-play some situations such as wanting to stay out late at a party or getting an extension for a piece of school work. One pair role-play and freeze the action so that the rest of the group can 'double' and explore alternative ways of handling negotiation.

Newspaper stories

What to do
The teacher collects newspaper headlines. The group members are then divided into pairs or small groups, each of which is given a headline. They must plan and enact a scene which they think fits the headline. Then they discuss the purpose of 'headlines' and the ways in which the media attract our interest/influence our thinking.

How this could be varied or developed
1. Collect and compare different headlines about the same story.
2. Discuss why different newspapers emphasise different aspects of a story.
3. Discuss what sorts of headlines attract pupil interest and why? What aspects of our nature is the headline appealing to?
4. The teacher can read a selection of news items from a paper and ask pairs or groups of pupils to think of a headline for each one. Groups then compare their suggested headlines.
5. The above activities can be extended into the realm of teenage magazines and developed to look at the issues surrounding teenage images and stereotypes.

Number call

What to do

Number the class consecutively round the circle, making sure that everyone has a number and can remember it. The leader then makes strong eye contact with one group member and calls out any number between 1 and the maximum number in the group. The person who has eye contact is not allowed to look away or say 'yes' or 'no' until the person to whom the number belongs 'rescues' him/her by calling out 'yes'.

The game highlights the need to be kind to one another and 'rescue' our class team. It also highlights the issues of comfortable and uncomfortable eye contact, the appropriateness of eye contact and its uses in social settings.

How it could be varied or developed

1. **The numbers can be 'thrown' across the circle. The person who 'catches' the number then 'throws' it to someone else, e.g. number one calls out 'One to seventeen', then seventeen says 'Seventeen to three' etc.**
2. **Add complications such as a rule that no number can be repeated and/or the number has to be sent to the opposite side of the circle, not to the person next door.**
3. **A development of this game is to add a noise by patting hands on knees. The noise makes the game much harder because it distracts the players and it is very hard to concentrate on two things at the same time. The group can then discuss the distractions that make it difficult to concentrate in lessons.**
4. **From variation 3 develop a discussion about distractions in class. Have a round 'I can't concentrate when . . .' and move the discussion on to common distractions in this class and ways of resolving them.**

Opting out

What to do

Participants are divided into groups of four. They are asked to think of a situation in which three members of the group are putting pressure on the fourth to join them in an activity/situation which the fourth does not want to do. The three persuaders use various tactics, e.g. persuasion, bullying, threats, bribes etc. Each group role-plays their situation.

Examples
- **A, B, C want D to join them in picking a fight with someone else.**
- **A, B, C want D to join them in playing truant.**
- **A, B, C want D to join them on a shoplifting spree.**
- **A, B, C want D to sneak out with them at night after bedtime.**
- **A, B, C want D to break into a scrap merchants yard with them to 'have some fun'.**

Check out

Encourage participants to try and really 'feel' their roles.

How this could be varied and developed

1. The teacher leads a discussion on the difficulties of dealing with peer pressure. If there are lots of views, the teacher could instigate a round of 'I find it difficult to resist when . . .'.

2. What makes them comply and what would help them to refuse?

3. Do any individuals want help with an issue involving peer pressure? Individuals in the group can suggest strategies to help deal effectively with peer pressure. Use the scripts 'Would it help if you . . .?', 'Would it help if I . . .?', 'Would it help if we . . .?' If an individual does not want help, keep the discussion more general, perhaps picking up from the initial role-plays.

Parental concerns

What to do

Participants work in pairs. They choose a situation of conflict that arises between them and one of their parents. They each take a turn to play the role of a parent then the child. The parent tells the child all the concerns s/he has about the child's behaviour, while the child justifies or excuses whatever the concern is.

How this could be varied or developed

1. Participants can discuss whether they consider parental concerns are usually justifiable. What should parents do about the concerns they have for their children's welfare?

2. How might the children allay their parent's concerns?

3. One or more of the role-plays could be shown to the whole group and 'doubling' used to find a variety of ways of thinking and responding. The teacher could play the child in one of the role-plays!

Pass the action

What to do

Any action can be passed round the circle from one person to the next as fast and as smoothly as possible. Mexican waves are popular and develop a sense of 'whole group' as the members cooperate in transferring the action. Passing a smile generates a lot of laughter.

How it could be varied

1. Passing actions, e.g. a handshake can be good for introducing touch into the group. Touch is associated with being liked and accepted; it can bring acceptance and warmth into the group.

2. An action can be 'activated' in the next person by gently touching them below the knee.

3. The group stands in a circle facing in one direction. The first person draws a simple design on the back of the next person. This design is then passed on round the circle and the end person draws it on to a piece of paper. A comparison is made between the end design and the initial one drawn by the first participant.

Pass the snake

What to do

Participants stand in an inward-facing circle. The teacher tells them they are going to mime passing 'objects' around the circle from one person to the next. The teacher chooses one player to mime passing a snake in an appropriate manner. After the snake has been passed several times, the teacher changes the 'object' and the game continues with the appropriate changes.

Examples of 'objects'

- hot plate of soup;
- heavy suitcase;
- sticky bun;
- foul smelling experiment.

How this can be varied or developed

1. Participants can form small groups of four or five and improvise a scene, passing one of the 'objects' as a starting point.
2. In the circle the group can discuss how we understand one another without words and the concentration required to read non-verbal signals in conversation.
3. Brainstorm times when it is essential that you can accurately read non-verbal cues.

Play the game

What to do

Participants sit in an inward-facing circle. Two or three participants leave the room. The remaining players decide on a 'rule' to play the game by. When the rule is established, the absent players return and take turns to question everyone in the circle about anything. All answers must abide by the agreed rule. The object of the game is to discover the rule and the people who are guessing can confer. NB Make sure that the rules do not become too complicated, especially at the beginning.

Examples

- Girls answer truthfully and boys do not.
- Anyone answering must cross his/her legs.
- All answers must include a specific word, e.g. 'perhaps'.

How this can be varied and developed

1. This game can lead to a discussion on rules and their purpose; why people keep them and why they break them.
2. What sort of rules are most beneficial and which are least?
3. Participants can consider rules in different contexts and circumstances as appropriate to the group's experience, e.g. in society, at home, at school, at work.
4. Can have a round of 'If I were in charge one rule I would make is . . .'.

Positive news

What to do

Participants are told to mingle with each other. Each person must say one genuine and positive thing to as many other people as possible. If the group is not able to do this yet, structure the activity by giving each person in the circle the letter A or B alternately. A and B make up a pair. When you want to change the pairs, ask all the 'A's to stand up and move clockwise to the fourth chair along and sit down. The person to their right is their new partner. NB Watch out for any pupils who find it particularly difficult to give a compliment.

Examples

- You have lovely blue eyes.
- I like your shoes.
- You're always friendly.
- I liked the way you spoke about . . .
- I really like the way you smile at me.

How this can be varied and developed

1. In the circle discuss why it is sometimes difficult to give or receive compliments.
2. Why is positive feedback important to people? For example, as an encouragement, to make them feel valued and to boost confidence.
3. Each person can set a target to give a compliment to someone every day this week and to say 'Thank you' when they receive a compliment.

Problem-solving

What to do

Start the game by asking the group to brainstorm problems. A brainstorm requires that every suggestion is accepted without comment. No-one may say that one person's idea is not a problem, even if it would not present a problem to them!

In groups of four, participants are given problem situations, which they must resolve as a group, by discussing what each member would do to help. At the end, each group can present their solution to the rest of the class.

Examples

1. The group is walking in remote countryside. It is dusk and getting cold. One member of the group falls over a cliff edge and is badly hurt. The territory is unfamiliar to the group.
2. You've lost something you borrowed from a friend. You promised to return it today and can't find it.
3. You've found out your brother/sister is taking drugs.
4. You don't know how to finish with your boy/girl friend.
5. A friend has started shoplifting.
6. You've been feeling unwell and are frightened you might have a serious illness.
7. You don't understand a piece of work, but don't want to appear stupid.

How this could be varied and developed

1. Participants can discuss panic situations; have a round of 'I tend to panic when . . .'.
2. Discuss the nature of panic. How do they think they would react?
3. Brainstorm ways of dealing with panic so that they can stay calm and think rationally.
4. Ask if any individual would like some help with a particular situation that causes them to panic. Ask the class to use the script 'Would it help if . . .?'.

Red Queen

What to do

The teacher supplies a pack of playing cards. Each participant is given a card (two of which are the Queen of Hearts and the Queen of Diamonds). Players must not name their cards out loud. The object of the game is to get rid of the red queens. Players approach one another and ask if they can swap cards. If the individual feels this is safe, they comply. If they think they might be given a red queen, they can refuse. However, each player has to make at least two swaps. After several minutes the teacher stops the game and the two players holding the red queens are out and sit down in the circle. The cards are collected in. Two 'safe' cards are removed and they are dealt out again. The game can continue for several more goes.

Check that players do swap and don't hang on to 'safe' cards.

How this could be varied and developed

1. The teacher leads a discussion on how pupils reacted when they held the red queens. Could they 'read' other players' expressions/body language to know if they held 'safe' cards or the queens? How daring were they in swapping cards?
2. Discussion can continue on how daring we are in life. What kind of risks do we take? How do we feel about taking on new challenges? How secure are we in the face of change? What prevents people from being more daring – look at lack of confidence, low self-esteem, physical fear etc.
3. The game can be repeated at a faster tempo where participants are not allowed to refuse a request to swap.
4. Change the rules so that each time the action stops, the two players holding the red queens gain a point.

Reflections

What to do

Participants work in pairs. One of the pair copies the action of the other as if s/he were a reflection in a mirror. The pair then swap roles. It is important that the participants make the movements slow and distinct so that the pair can synchronize movements as much as possible.

How this can be varied or developed

1. Make up groups of four. One pair agrees and performs a cooperative movement and the second pair mirrors the action.

2. Return to the circle and discuss how hard/easy the game was. Could they 'read' their partner's mind and anticipate the movement that would follow? What did they have to concentrate on most?

3. This can be developed into a counselling type exercise where pairs have a discussion and subtly mirror one another's body movements in order to enhance empathy, e.g. If one person looks fed up while recounting an incident – his/her partner 'mirrors' that emotion, using facial expression, body stance etc.

4. Are there situations in life when it is important to be able to 'read' what will happen next?

5. Discuss times when an ability to 'read' the situation accurately would enable you to intervene and change the course of things before a crisis developed. Questions 4 and 5 may lead to some role-play of situations the pupils have raised and using the 'doubling' technique to explore different ways of intervening before there is a crisis.

Ring on a string

What to do

The teacher supplies a length of string and a ring. The participants sit close together, i.e. with their shoulders touching, in an inward-facing circle. A piece of string is cut long enough to stretch around the circle. A ring is threaded on to the string and the two ends tied together to form a continuous circle. One participant leaves the room and the remaining people hold the string with both hands palms downwards. They covertly pass the ring along the string from one person to the next. The absent player returns and must guess which player is holding the ring. Other players pretend to pass the ring to confuse the 'detective'. When a correct guess is made, another 'detective' is chosen and leaves the room while the ring is passed to a different place in the circle. NB It might be advisable to limit the number of guesses to three after which a new detective is chosen so that players don't get bored if someone has difficulty locating the ring.

How this could be varied or developed

1. Participants form two teams which stand facing each other, shoulder touching shoulder, hands behind their backs. Each team has a small object which they pass backwards and forwards along the line. Each team takes turns to guess or pass the object and every participant has a go at guessing which member of the opposite team has the object. The player is allowed two guesses and, if correct, his/her team receives a point. The game is played in silence, but participants try to confuse the person who is guessing with facial expressions, pretending to pass the object etc.

2. In a circle, the group can discuss situations where good teamwork is beneficial. What qualities make a good team member?

Saying sorry

What to do
The teacher has a selection of errors and misdemeanors. Participants work in pairs. Each participant chooses a situation from the selection and 'apologises' for it to his/her partner. The teacher tells the participants to choose initially a situation they might normally apologise for and then one which they would find difficult to apologise for.

Examples
- You deliberately ignored someone.
- You accidentally break someone's window.
- You forgot you have arranged to meet someone.
- You made an unkind remark about someone which they learned about.
- You were rude to someone.

How this could be varied and developed
1. Participants can discuss why or when they might find it difficult to apologise. Suggested round: 'I find it difficult to apologise when . . .'.
2. What are the pros and cons of apologising?
3. What might make it easier for them to apologise? Suggested round: 'I find it easier to apologise if . . .'.

Setbacks

What to do
Participants set up an obstacle course of chairs, books, bags etc. They take turns to negotiate the course, first on one leg, then backwards etc. (This can be done in groups of two or three if there is sufficient space.)

How this can be varied and developed
1. In the circle, the group brainstorms the irritating things that make progress around school more difficult for them, e.g. no locker, heavy bags, too long a queue.
2. Individuals can ask for the group's help in coping with difficulties.
3. Circle discussion about physical disability could immediately follow this game. What negative effects does disability bring? Could there be any positive effects? How do other people treat those with physical disability?

Similarities and differences

What to do
The teacher starts off by choosing some aspect of the group which is common to several members such as, 'All those who have laces in their shoes change places.' The statements can change from totally non-threatening, observable similarities to more personal disclosures such as 'Everyone who likes chocolate change places' or 'Everyone who dislikes their middle name.' Once the game is established, a chair is

removed from the circle so that one person is left in the middle. The person left in the middle then chooses the next similarity or difference.

Rules
- To get as far across the circle and away from your chair as possible.
- Not to push into anyone.
- To be honest about your preferences or dislikes.
- Not to be left in the middle.

How it could be varied or developed
1. In the circle, discuss the importance of having things in common with other people.
2. Extend the discussion to belonging to families, social groups, communities. What are the benefits and what are the responsibilities of being part of these different groups?

Tease

What to do
The teacher has a selection of situations in which someone is teased. In groups of four, participants are given a situation which they role play, each member taking on a different character, e.g. A – teaser, B – victim, C – observer, D – friend of either A or B. They can then swap roles. The repetition of a scenario with different people taking the different roles tends to release more imagination and a richer role-play. NB Encourage participants to try and feel empathy with 'victims'.

Examples
- A teases B about new hairstyle.
- A teases B about his/her name.
- A teases B about way he/she talks.
- A teases B, because B has spots.
- A teases B about being stupid.

How this could be varied and developed
1. The teacher leads a discussion on teasing. Is it always malicious or sometimes affectionate?
2. How can the victim respond effectively to stop the teasing? Brainstorm effective methods of dealing with unwanted teasing. One of the earlier role-play situations can be used as a basis for exploring different ways of dealing with teasing.
3. Discuss why some people are persistent teasers/victims?

Things in common

What to do
Four fruits are chosen and participants are each given the name of a fruit in order round the circle, e.g. apples, oranges, pears, bananas, apples etc. Everyone sits down in the circle and the teacher calls out a fruit. All the people who have that fruit name must change places. When 'fruit bowl' is called, everyone changes places.

How this could be varied and extended

1. The names given to each class member can be from any group of objects, e.g. vehicles such as cars, lorries, motorbikes, vans and all traffic or countries such as England, Scotland, Wales and Northern Ireland and United Kingdom. The possibilities are endless and the group can create their own categories.

2. The group mixes freely and the teacher calls out a category. Any person who fits that category has to find a partner in the same category, e.g. Anyone who has a birthday in September, anyone with brown eyes etc. When a pair has been formed, they both score a point and participants keep a tally of their score.

3. In the circle discuss the importance of sharing things in common.

4. Discuss the groups of people you belong to where you share something in common, e.g. your family which may share the same name, or the same house. Your community may live in the same area, use the same community hall etc. Your school has the same teachers, the same building etc.

5. Are there responsibilities that are attached to being part of a group?

Touchdown

What to do

Divide the group into pairs. Depending on the size of the group, divide the pairs into several teams, e.g. four teams with three pairs in each team. The teacher explains that s/he will call a number and the pairs in each team have to devise *different* ways of placing that number of body parts on the floor, e.g. if the number is three, one pair could stand with three feet touching the ground between them. The next pair in the team might kneel with three knees touching the ground between them. The next pair might have one person standing on one foot holding their partner's feet off the ground as in a wheelbarrow race. The first team to achieve *three different positions* wins a point.

How this could be varied or developed

1. The teams have to negotiate the different methods of touching the ground without speaking, using non-verbal communication skills.
2. The team designates one leader who has to make the decisions and everyone else must do as they are told, no matter whether they agree or disagree. The role of leader is rotated round the group.
3. Follow activity 2 with a discussion about how it feels to be responsible for the decision-making and how it feels to have to follow instructions even when you think you have a better idea.
4. Open forum could offer opportunity for members to look at situations when they have to follow instructions even when they disagree and strategies for coping with the accompanying feelings.

Who are you?

What to do

The group stands or sits in a circle and, in pairs, they think of a positive adjective that begins with the same letter as their first name. e.g. 'Smashing Sally' or 'Wonderful Wayne' etc. It is important to ensure that positive adjectives are used. Once everyone has thought of a positive alliterative adjective, each person, in turn says his/her name preceded by the positive adjective.

How it can be varied or developed

1. Each person says his/her name accompanied by a verb and an action, e.g. 'Mountaineering Mary' said while the person performs a mime of mountaineering.
2. A ball or beanbag can be thrown across the circle to different people. The person who catches it has to say his/her name either with or without the adjective. Or once the group gets to know one another's names, the thrower has to use the name of the person they throw to.

3. A ball or beanbag or soft toy can be thrown across the circle from one person to another accompanied by the script 'Hi, Smashing Sally, I'm Wonderful Wayne.' If anyone forgets the name of another group member, they can say 'Hi, I'm Wonderful Wayne, what's your name please?'

4. A ball of string or wool can be thrown to named people, so that it unravels and creates a web. The wool ensures that every person is included and there is a visual picture of 'group' at the end when everyone is joined together.

You're positive

What to do

Participants sit in an inward-facing circle. One person is asked to leave the room and the teacher asks for several positive statements about that person from any member of the group. When the person returns, the teacher repeats each statement asking him/her to guess who said each one. The teacher must ensure that no negative reactions occur if the person makes an incorrect guess, e.g. 'I wouldn't say that about you because I think you're ugly!' You can only play this when the group has built up a good rapport and ethos.

How this can be varied or developed

1. If group members are as yet unable to make three positive statements about individuals, discussion can take place so that the whole group comes up with positive statements which are written down and given as a present to the person outside the room on their return.

2. In the circle discuss how hearing positive statements affects people.

3. What effect do positive statements have on self-confidence, relationships with others and work?

4. Targets can be set to look for positive things to say to people in the next week.

Zoom – Eek

One pupil starts a car going around the circle by saying 'Zoom' and turning his or her head quickly to the person on the right. The next person repeats this action and it continues around the circle until a pupils says 'Eek'. The car then changes direction and the 'Zoom' sound goes the other way until the next 'Eek'. At first the teacher can say 'Zoom' and 'Eek' and once the game is established, the pupils can determine the direction of the car's movement themselves.

Sometimes one section of the circle will monopolise the action by their use of the 'Eek'. If this happens, it can be highlighted with a discussion on consideration. Another strategy is to issue each pupil with an 'Eek' card. Once they have used their 'Eek', they must put the card into the centre of the circle. They can learn to use their 'Eek' card strategically and eventually all the 'Eeks' will be used up.

16 Rounds

The round, already described in Chapter 12, is used to make sure that everyone has the opportunity to speak and be listened to. In this model of Circle Time, a speaking object is used as a visual symbol of respectful listening. When someone holds the object, they have the opportunity to speak and everyone else listens. The rule is that no one may interrupt the person holding the speaking object. Even the teacher must get up, move across the circle, touch the object and apologise to the person who is speaking before s/he may interrupt the process. The round gives a very strong message about the respect afforded to someone when they speak. It is also a democratic process as everyone has a turn. The right to say 'I pass' means that an individual can choose whether to take part or to sit quietly. At the end of the round the last person to speak says 'Does anyone who passed want a turn?' If someone who has not already contributed to the round has now thought of something they want to say, the object is taken to them and they have an opportunity to speak.

Members of the group are always encouraged to take responsibility for what they say and whether or not they contribute. Very often a round has a scripted sentence stem which begins with an 'I' statement, e.g. 'I feel happy when . . .', 'In my spare time I like to . . .'. The use of 'I', and 'My' are important to assertive communication and encourage ownership of and responsibility for thoughts, feelings and actions.

Getting to know you: paired discussions and rounds

Discussion	Where did you live at the age of 7? How many brothers and sisters did you have?
Round	'When I was seven, I lived in . . . I had . . . brothers and . . . sisters.
Or	'This is . . . When s/he was seven s/he lived . . . and s/he had . . . brothers and . . . sisters.
Discussion	What was the happiest moment in your life?
Round	'The happiest moment of my life was . . .'
Discussion	What is the greatest regret of your life?
Round	'My greatest regret is . . .'
Discussion	Which room in your house do you like best and why?
Round	'My favourite room is . . . because . . .'
Discussion	What is one thing you want to do next week?
Round	'Next week I will . . .'
Discussion	If you had a machine that would work only once, what point in the future or in history would you visit?
Round	'I would use my machine to visit . . ., because . . .'
Discussion	If you could take a tablet that would enable you to live to 1000 years, would you take it and why/why not?
Round	'I would/would not take the tablet because . . .'
Discussion	What was the best/worst experience of your week.
Round	'The best thing that happened this week was . . .'
	'The worst thing that happened this week was . . .'
Discussion	If you could go anywhere in the world for three days, where would you go and why?
Round	'I would go to . . ., because . . .'
Discussion	How do you relax?
Round	'I relax by . . .'
Discussion	What is your favourite type of music/song?
Round	'My favourite music is . . .'
Discussion	If you could not fail, what would you like to do?
Round	'If I could not fail, I would . . .'
Discussion	Name a present you will never forget.
Round	'A present I will never forget is . . .'

Discussion   When was the last time you made a mistake. How did you feel?
Round   'When I make a mistake, I feel . . .'

Rounds about feelings

There has been much research in recent years on what makes people do well in life. The traditional view is that bright people – those with a high IQ – do well and those with a lower IQ score do less well and since intelligence is genetically fixed, there is nothing we can do about it. More and more research demonstrates this to be untrue. We could all cite examples of those with high IQ who have foundered and those with modest IQ who have done exceedingly well. Other factors seem to be at work. These factors have been called emotional intelligence, and include self-control, zeal, persistence and the ability to motivate oneself. These skills can be taught to pupils, giving them a better chance to use whatever intellectual potential their genetic make-up may have given them.

The following rounds are designed to encourage recognition and ownership of emotions. They involve 'I' statements and connect an emotion with a situation that engenders those feelings.

The group is given the sentence stem and a minute or two to think about the feelings and situations. The speaking object is given to the first person or a volunteer who is brave enough to start and the round begins.

'I feel happy when . . .'	'I feel sad when . . .'
'One thing that makes me angry is . . .'	'I get scared when . . .'
'The most frustrating thing for me is . . .'	'I am always excited when . . .'
'I feel really safe when . . .'	'My favourite person is . . .'
'The possession I love the most is . . .'	'Silence makes me feel . . .'
'The person I admire the most is . . .'	'I hate it when . . .'
'I feel pushed when . . .'	'I like to be alone when . . .'
'A sound that makes me happy is . . .'	'I hate being alone when . . .'

The list is endless and can be designed to suit any topic when it is important to access feelings.

17 Drama and role-play

	Cooperation	Concentration	Imagination	Listening	Speaking	Observation	Creativity	Thinking	Self-affirmation	Self-esteem	Assertiveness	Appreciation	Laughter/fun	Empathy	Self-disclosure	Confidence
Adverbs			•		•		•	•		•				•	•	
Committees	•			•	•			•		•	•					•
Defusing anger	•			•	•							•		•		
Dramatic scenes	•		•	•	•											
Emotions		•		•		•				•				•	•	•
Factories	•		•				•						•			
Freeze			•	•	•			•								•
Guess the scene			•										•			
If the cap fits			•						•	•	•		•			•
Improvisation 1	•		•				•			•	•				•	•
Improvisation 2	•		•				•			•	•				•	•
Instructions					•			•								•
Muscial scenes			•	•			•									
Opposites	•		•	•	•	•	•						•			
Party-goers			•	•	•	•							•			•
Proverbs		•	•													
Racing charades		•	•										•			
Scene change	•	•	•				•									
Scenes				•	•		•	•						•	•	•
Sign language		•	•			•	•									
Silent movies		•	•			•	•									
Social gatherings			•	•	•	•						•		•		
Story roundabout		•	•		•		•	•					•	•		•
The journey			•		•		•					•		•		
The waiting room			•	•	•									•		•
Theme pictures	•		•	•	•		•	•								
Yes and no				•	•	•								•		•

Figure 17.1 Key to drama and role-play for Circle Time

Adverbs

What to do

You will need a prepared list of adverbs. Participants are told that they must try to walk, think and speak in the manner of each adverb. The teacher tells them they can mingle with each other, greet one another and hold conversations. The teacher changes the adverb at regular intervals. NB Encourage participants to really try and feel the adverb.

Examples of adverbs
- aggressively
- shyly
- sorrowfully
- impatiently
- joyfully

How this could be varied and developed
Participants can discuss how emotions affect their behaviour and how this might influence other people's responses to them.

Committees

What to do
You will need a prepared list of different types of committee. In groups of 4–6, participants are told they are committee members of a meeting. Each group is given a 'situation' to role-play. Participants must try and think of all the difficulties, needs, circumstances, possibilities and concerns. They can elect a chairperson to oversee proceedings. NB Encourage participants to adopt a character type and act/react accordingly.

Examples
- members of the school council with £500 to spend on extra equipment;
- members of a committee discussing taking handicapped people on holiday;
- members of a committee discussing what venues to take foreign visitors to.

How this could be varied and developed
1. Participants can discuss the problems they encountered. What qualities do they think make a good and effective team of committee members? For example, able to cooperate, able to listen, able to negotiate.
2. Are any school situations similar to a committee? Are there times in school when we need the same skills as committee members?
3. Have a round of 'I am a good team member when I . . .'.

Defusing anger

What to do
Prepare a list of confrontational situations. The teacher has a selection of situations that have provoked anger. Pupils work in pairs A and B role-play how the angry person would behave and how the partner might respond, first in a negative way and then in a positive way to resolve the situation. Pupils then choose a new situation and reverse roles. NB Encourage participants to try and respond as they would if they really were angry.

Examples
- A is spreading untrue rumours about B.
- A has copied B's idea for a piece of work.
- A has tried to steal B's girl/boyfriend.
- A has 'told tales' on B, resulting in B getting into trouble.
- A is angry with B for not tidying up as agreed.
- A has borrowed something from B and ruined it.

How this could be varied and developed
1. Have a round 'When I get angry I . . .'. This will encourage an understanding of a range of responses to anger.
2. Pupils discuss the best ways of dealing with someone else's anger.
3. What might escalate anger and what defuses it?
4. Pupils discuss ways of defusing their own anger so that it becomes less destructive to self/others.

Dramatic scenes

What to do
Prepare sets of 'characters' on separate pieces of paper and place them in containers with one set for each group of pupils in the class. Pupils are divided into groups of 4–6 participants. Each person picks a character out of their container and the group makes up a scene involving all the characters in a meaningful way. NB Be aware of any shy participants who might need encouragement to contribute more fully.

Examples of characters

• doctor	• tramp	• plumber
• vicar	• blind person	• hairdresser
• sports person	• builder	

How this can be varied and developed
1. Participants can discuss how easy/difficult it was to involve all the characters in one scene.
2. What problems arose from working as a group? How did the group resolve them?

Emotions

What to do
The teacher needs a prepared list of emotions. Pupils are divided into small groups and each group is given two emotions. The groups are asked to think up and enact a 'scene' which involves both emotions. NB Encourage participants to use both emotions plausibly.

Examples
- panic – anger
- embarrassment – impatience
- grief – weariness
- amusement – triumph

How this could be varied and developed
1. On a large sheet of paper or the board, pupils can list emotions under the headings 'negative emotions', 'positive emotions' and discuss what effect they have on us.
2. Do some emotions fit into both lists?
3. Can negative emotions be made into positive ones?
4. What factors/situations make it difficult for group members to control their emotions? This could be followed by a round 'I find it difficult to control my emotions when . . .'.
5. What strategies can members of the group suggest for managing their emotions?

Factories

What to do
In groups of 4–6, the participants are told that they work on a production line in a factory. Each group decides on its 'product' and manufacturing process, so that every member has a job to do on the production line. The groups then mime their factories 'at work'. They can give a commentary on the process, as it happens. NB Encourage participants to divide up the 'action' evenly.

How this could be varied and developed
1. Participants can discuss the benefits of working together to achieve a goal.
2. How are people uncooperative?
3. Why might people not cooperate with others? Suggested round: 'I find it difficult to cooperate in groupwork when . . .'.
4. What helps people to be cooperative? Suggested round: 'I find it easier to work in groups when . . .'.

Freeze

What to do
You may wish to have produced suitable 'starting points' on cards or pieces of paper before the start of the lesson. Participants form groups of 5–6. The teacher gives a 'starting point' from which the groups develop a scene deciding their own characters. One member of each group stands 'on the sidelines' watching the scene and notes how it is developing. When the teacher calls 'freeze' the players stop, and the 'bystander' replaces any one of the characters, but must play it differently so that the story line changes. NB Participants could offer suggestions to any one who is 'stuck' about a character change.

Examples of starting points
- a car accident
- a shop display falls down
- a window is broken
- a horse escapes from a field
- a knock at the door

How this could be varied and developed

Participants can discuss how different 'characters' can alter group dynamics and change situations.

Guess the scene

What to do

Participants are divided into groups of 5–6. One member of each group leaves the room. The remaining players think of a situation around which they devise a simple scene. The absent players are invited back and each watch their group's performance. They can then question the group but are only given 'yes' or 'no' answers until they guess what is happening in the scene. A different player then leaves the room and the group thinks of a new situation.

How this can be varied and developed

1. Participants can talk about real-life situations. Have they ever misconstrued a situation?
2. What gave them the wrong impression?
3. How did they react then and afterwards?
4. Some of the situations that pupils cite could be role-played and the reactions explored to provide a range of possible responses.

If the cap fits . . .

What to do

Teacher has a black dustbin bag of different hats. Participants are invited to take a hat out of the bag and put it on. They must walk, talk and act in a manner appropriate to the hat they are wearing. NB Encourage shy participants to lose their inhibitions.

Examples of hats
- policeman's helmet
- riding hat
- woolly multi-coloured hat
- bowler hat
- mob cap
- sombrero

119

How this could be varied or developed

1. Participants can discuss whether they consider that certain clothes affect people's behaviour, e.g. military uniform or a particularly flamboyant outfit.
2. What do people choose personal clothes for? For example to convey an 'image'.
3. The discussion can be extended to particular events when pupils choose their own clothes, e.g. non-uniform days. How do pupils feel about choosing their outfit for a non-uniform day or a school outing?
4. Why do we have school uniform?

Improvisation 1

What to do

The teacher needs to have collected together a selection of everyday objects. Participants are divided into groups of four. Each group is given an object, which has to become the focus of a scene. Each group makes up a story around their object, which must involve all members of the group. NB Encourage all group members to be actively involved.

Examples of objects

- telephone
- knife
- spade
- jewellery box
- brief case

How this could be varied and developed

Participants can discuss how inanimate objects can affect or influence their everyday lives in different ways.

Examples

- Television – informative, entertaining, but can be too dominating.
- Carrier bag – useful and can also be used to enhance image

Improvisation 2

What to do

The teacher needs a selection of everyday objects such as those in the list below. Participants are divided into groups of four. Each group is given an object of no apparent use and must devise a 'use' and build a scene around their object.

Examples of objects

- plastic ring
- piece of cloth
- cardboard tube
- wooden block
- length of rope

How this could be varied and developed

1. Participants can discuss 'being inventive' and how real inventions might happen.
2. This could lead on to the ethics of inventions and how they can bring both benefit and harm, e.g. cars, drugs.

Instructions

What to do

The teacher has a selection of 'tasks'. Participants work in pairs. Each player chooses a 'task' which s/he must explain in detailed stages to his/her partner. The partner must then report back the details as accurately as possible.

Examples of tasks
- laying a fire
- making a pot of tea
- making and baking a cake
- dyeing one's hair
- 'cutting out' material from a paper pattern
- wrapping and sending a parcel

How this could be varied and developed

1. Participants can discuss what, in a teaching situation, makes it easier/more difficult for them to listen effectively. This could be followed by a round: 'I find it hard to listen when . . .' or 'I find it hard to hear when . . .' or 'I find it hard to concentrate on what the teacher is saying when . . .'.
2. What makes it easier/more difficult to give precise, informative directions?

Musical scenes

What to do

Have a prepared selection of music and a tape recorder or CD player available. Participants work in small groups of 4–6. The teacher has a selection of different types of music on tape or CD. The groups are instructed to listen to a piece of music and then develop a short 'scene' suggested to them by the music. The teacher then plays a different piece and the groups perform another scene. NB Tell participants it might help if they close their eyes while the music is playing and give their imaginations free rein.

How this could be varied and developed

1. How often did the music initially suggest the same scene to group members and how often were their 'imaginings' different?
2. Participants can discuss whether one sort of music is 'better' than another and the influence and effect of music on people and why people have different musical tastes.

Opposites

What to do

You will need a prepared list of characters and situations. Participants form pairs. Each pair is given opposite characters and the whole group is given a situation. Pairs improvise a scene within that situation. They then swap characters and form a new pair. The teacher gives a new situation. NB Watch out that one partner does not dominate the scenes every time.

Examples of characters	*Examples of situations*
Grumpy – happy	In a shop
Timid – bold	In a bus queue
Anxious – happy-go-lucky	On a train
Rich – poor	In a restaurant
Serious – joker	At the theatre

How this can be varied and developed

1. Pairs can be invited to show their improvisations to the rest of the group and the other group member can guess what characters they are playing.
2. Participants can discuss what 'clues' they get from people's behaviour, which tell them about their personalities.

Party-goers

What to do

Have a prepared list of party characters. As a class or in smaller groups each participant is given a character to role-play at a party. Participants are told they must talk and act as their name suggests. Try and give participants characters very different from their own. NB Encourage the less confident participants to overcome their inhibitions.

Examples of characters

- Larry Loud
- Tina Timid
- Brian Bossy
- Sarah Secretive
- Danny Doubtful

How this could be varied and developed

1. Ask participants to give themselves a name that aptly describes their own character.
2. Do the other participants think their choice is a suitable one?
3. Would they prefer a different one?

If any names were negative ask participants to think of an alternative positive one.

Proverbs

What to do

You will need a prepared list of proverbs, perhaps written individually on slips of paper. Working in small groups, participants are given a proverb to build a scene around. They are instructed that their scene must portray the meaning of the proverb, but must not be a direct play around the words of the proverb. Groups perform their scenes to the other participants who are then invited to guess what the proverb was.

Examples
- All that glitters is not gold.
- Don't count your chickens before they've hatched.
- Blood is thicker than water.
- A stitch in time saves nine.

How this could be varied and developed
- Participants can discuss the value of proverbs.
- Why, do they think, they are seldom used today?

Racing charades

What to do
The teacher has a prepared list of well-known book, film and television titles. The class is divided into two teams which go to opposite ends of the room. The teacher sits in the middle with the list of titles. A player from each team goes to the teacher who whispers the first title to them. They race back to their team and mime the title (they can state or mime whether it is a book/film/TV show). As soon as the team has guessed a title, another player goes to the teacher to say the correct answer and receive the next whispered title. The winning team is the one which guesses all the titles first. No verbal clues are allowed.

If a team gets really stuck, they can go to the next clue and come back to the problem clue at the end.

How this could be varied and developed
1. Two teams can play challenge charades where they sit in rows facing the opposite team. Players from each team take turns to challenge a named opponent to guess the mimes they perform. If the 'opponent' answers correctly his/her team receives two points. If s/he needs help from other team members they only receive one point. Players must choose a different named opponent each time to prevent them from continuously choosing someone who is not very good at guessing.
2. Pupils discuss how they found the first or second game. Did they find it difficult to communicate or to think of appropriate mimes? Did they feel embarrassed or nervous about performing the mimes? Are there situations in life where they have to 'perform' in front of others? How might they cope better with the fear of performing?

Scene change

What to do
You will need a prepared list of key words. Participants mingle freely. The teacher calls a number from two to six and participants form groups of the number called. The teacher then calls a 'keyword' and each group has to improvise a scene around that word. After an interval of time the teacher instructs participants to mingle again and calls a different number and keyword.

Examples of keywords
- river
- hospital
- uncle
- soup
- carpet

How this could be varied and developed
Participants can develop one of the scenes into a short play.

Scenes

What to do
Divide the group into sets of four. Each set will have a cast of four characters. The teacher provides sets of photocopied 'characters' for each group (see below). The group then rehearses a five-minute scene in the context of the scenario given below. As far as possible, the pupils are to let the scene develop spontaneously according to their characters' actions and responses and with as little discussion as possible.

Scenario
The four characters have arrived at a large, roomy house in the middle of the countryside for an evening course on meditation. No one greeted them on their arrival, but as the door was ajar, they went in. They have been sitting in the lounge for over half an hour. Their host, Dr Barari, is nowhere to be seen and the house seems deserted. The scene opens with Rachel saying, 'I'm getting a bit worried. What on earth can have happened to Dr Barani? What should we do?'

Characters

Rachel (or Daniel)	Mid-thirties, lives with mother. Very nervous type. Constantly worrying and expecting the worst. Physically timid, easily intimidated by others.
Josh	Mid-twenties. Spends life travelling round the world doing occasional work when necessary. Very laid-back, inclined to be lazy and self-centred. Not really bothered about other people's feelings. Doesn't like spending money.
Brad (or Patsy)	Early thirties. Ex-army. Very fit and athletic. Somewhat impetuous; likes to act first, think afterwards. Inclined to be bossy and a know-all, but is also considerate of others.
Daisy	Late teens. Done some modelling. A bit silly and vain. Likes to exaggerate everything and sometimes even tells lies to make herself or situations seem more important or exciting. Not very practical and usually unaware of other people's feelings, i.e. always says the wrong thing.

How this could be varied or developed
1. Pupils return to the circle and each group performs their scene for the rest of the class.
2. After all the scenes have been performed the participants are asked how similar they thought each character was in the different sets. What do they think accounted for the differences?
3. The teacher can ask all the players of one character how they saw that character in

their mind's eye. What did s/he look like? What kind of dress did s/he wear? What mannerisms did s/he have?

4. Discuss what further instructions would have been necessary to make the players interpret the character in a more similar way.

5. The same characters can be used in a variety of scenarios, e.g.
   - A coach trip in a foreign country. The coach driver is taken ill and cannot drive . . .
   - A plane crash in an area of desert. The four characters have survived the crash and are trying to survive until they are rescued.

Sign language

What to do
The teacher gives each participant a prepared question. The participants are put in pairs and each person looks at their questions then, in silence, takes turns to mime the question and a response (players can check verbally afterwards to see if they have properly understood the question and response). Both members of the pair can mime his/her questions then move on to another player and repeat the process. NB Make sure that shy participants do join in.

Examples
   - Can I have six eggs please?
   - Where is the restaurant?
   - What time does the cinema open?
   - Would you like to come to the disco with me?

How this could be varied and developed
1. Participants can discuss how difficult/easy they found the game.
2. Did their mimes improve with practice?
3. What other 'signs' did they use? For example, facial expressions.
4. What do they think it would be like to rely on sign language as deaf people do?

Silent movies

What to do
Participants work in groups of 4–6. They are instructed to think up a story, which they perform in mime only. They must take particular care to try and ensure that their actions explicitly reveal the story line. Groups can take turns to perform their scenes. The watching group members are then invited to describe what they thought was happening.

How this could be varied and developed
1. Participants can discuss the differences between watching mimed and spoken scenes. What 'clues' help them to make sense of mimed action?
2. What differences do they think there are with regards to characters and action between radio and television plays?

Social gatherings

What to do

The teacher has a selection of pre-written cards each naming a different group of people. In groups of four, participants are given one card and instructed to imagine that they are members of that group at a social gathering. Through role-play, they imagine what they might talk about and how they would behave.

Examples

- old people
- young people
- New Age travellers
- politicians

How this could be varied and developed

Participants can discuss what sorts of things affect our interests, priorities, discussions etc.

Story roundabout

What to do

The class is divided into groups of five or six. A selection of situations (examples given below) are written on card and one is given to each group. They are given some time to discuss characters and story line. The groups are then instructed that they will begin an improvisation involving four of their members. The fifth (and sixth) member observes the improvisation. On the teacher's command, the 'acting' stops and the observer takes over the role of one of the characters, who becomes the observer. The action then continues. At regular intervals the teacher stops the action and the observer takes over one of the roles. This is done on a rotational basis so that participants play several different characters (i.e. players 1, 2, 3, 4, observer 5; 5 takes over role of 1 who becomes observer; 1 then takes over role of 2 who becomes the observer; 2 then takes over role of 3 who becomes the observer etc.).

How it could be developed or varied

1. At the end of the time, participants can discuss how easy/difficult it was to assume different roles.
2. Do they think 'playing' different roles can help in real life?
3. Did different players interpret the same role in different ways?

Situations for story roundabout

1. The scene takes place in the school canteen. It involves a conflict between the midday supervisor and the pupils. You can decide what role you put the teacher in. S/he could be an authority figure, an arbitrator, or they could ignore the situation. In your scenario, note how the supervisor, the pupils and the teacher feels.

   Characters
   - midday supervisor
   - two pupils
   - a teacher

2. **The scene takes place on a sandy beach and involves a conflict of interests between a sunbather who wants some peace and children who want to play. Let the conflict develop. You can resolve it, or leave it as a conflict of interests, but notice how you feel when you play the various roles.**

Characters
- sunbather
- two people running about playing 'ball'
- person in deckchair who is reading a paper

3. **The scene takes place on a factory floor. One worker's sleeve becomes caught in a machine. Try to capture the feelings of confusion, panic and decision-making. Note how you feel at each stage of the drama.**

Characters
- worker whose sleeve gets caught in a machine
- fellow worker
- foreman/woman
- factory owner

4. **The scene takes place at an important function. The waiter spills wine over the visiting dignitary just before s/he makes an important speech. Imagine the feelings each character would have and develop the scene in any way you like.**

Characters

- visiting dignitary about to make a speech
- journalist
- organizer
- waiter who spilt the wine

The Journey

What to do
Divide the class into groups of five or six. Each group is given a 'journey' from the list below. On each journey there are six characters (one character is omitted if their group is smaller). The pupils are asked to develop a scene in which the characters view the journey, react to incidents on the way and to one another according to their roles.

Characters
- fussy lady
- sports person
- physically disabled person
- old person
- nervous man
- know-it-all

Examples of 'journeys'

- a stormy sea crossing in a small boat
- a trek through jungle undergrowth
- a mountain ascent
- a highjack during an aeroplane flight
- a trek across a snowy wasteland

How it could be developed

1. Encourage participants to try and really think and react as their characters.
2. In the circle, discuss how playing other characters can help them become more sensitive and tolerant towards other people.
3. This could be moved on into an open forum on specific situations that bring misunderstanding and include a round: 'I feel misunderstood when . . .'.
4. Pupils could brainstorm strategies for coping with situations when they are misunderstood.

The waiting room

What to do

This can be done in groups of six upwards. The teacher has a selection of pre-written cards naming different characters. Each participant is given a character and instructed to try and think, behave, converse as this character would. They are in a waiting room and must act and react to the other characters in the manner of their own character. At the beginning each participant states his/her character. NB Participants can offer suggestions to any member of their own group who has difficulty in developing their character.

Examples of characters

- an old person
- a vicar
- a tramp
- a 'hippie' or New Age traveller
- a young child
- a blind person

How this could be varied and developed

1. The group can discuss preconceived ideas we have about different character types and how our beliefs affect us and other people.
2. How can generalisations be dangerous?

Theme pictures

What to do

The teacher has a selection of newspaper/magazine pictures of people involved in different situations. Participants are divided into groups of 4–6 and each group is given a photograph and asked to devise a scene which they think reflects what is happening in the photo. NB Encourage participants to develop their characters.

How this could be varied and developed

1. Participants can discuss how much 'information' they can get from photos.
2. What sort of visual 'clues' do they look for?
3. Do they interpret all the clues in the same way?
4. Can photographs be misleading?
5. What kind of publications may produce misleading pictures and what is their use?

Yes and no

What to do
You will need a prepared list of subjects. Participants work in pairs. They are given or they choose a subject about which they must argue, one for and one against. The teacher explains that, regardless of personal opinions, they must really try to think and feel as the role demands. After a time the teacher tells them to reverse roles (trying to reverse their thoughts and feelings as well) and continue the argument.

Examples of subjects
- homework
- competitive sports
- school uniforms
- single sex schools
- smoking in restaurants
- violence on television

How this could be varied and developed
1. Participants can discuss the value of changing roles.
2. Discuss whether acknowledging other people's opinions and how putting themselves into other people's shoes could help resolve disputes.

18 Quizzes

	Cooperation	Concentration	Imagination	Listening	Speaking	Observation	Creativity	Thinking	Self-affirmation	Self-esteem	Assertiveness	Appreciation	Laughter/fun	Empathy	Self-disclosure	Confidence
Alphabet game	•	•	•					•					•			
Collage quiz	•	•	•			•		•					•			
Guess the country	•	•		•				•					•			
Match the adverts	•	•				•		•					•			
Missing pieces	•	•				•		•								
Pairs quiz								•								
Picture stories	•	•	•	•			•	•								
Treasure hunt		•	•			•		•					•			

Figure 18.1 Key to quizzes

Alphabet game

What to do
The teacher prepares two sets of cards of the most commonly used letters. Participants form two teams and each team member has a card. (Some pupils may have to have two cards.) The teacher calls out words and the first team to spell out the word (stand with letters in correct sequence) receives a point. If there are an unequal number in the teams, one participant will have two letters. NB If any participants have a problem with spelling, team-mates can help.

Examples
If there are thirty participants the teacher could use the following sets of letters:

    A E I O U B D G L M N P R S T

Words
slot, mime, badger, grab, punt, dune, made, pilot

How this could be varied and developed
At opposite ends of the room the two teams think of the six most difficult words they can and the teacher notes them down in two separate lists. The teams reassemble in the middle. The teacher reads out the first word that team A thought of and team B puts the letters they have in the correct order for the word, leaving out any letters they do not have. The teacher uses a stopwatch to see how long it takes to complete

the word and notes it down. S/he then gives team A the first word team B thought of. The team that takes the least time to spell a word is the winner.

Collage quiz

What to do
The teacher prepares a collage of magazine photographs/advertisements on a large sheet of card. Participants work in pairs and have a prepared list of questions to answer. They answer as many as possible in a set time. NB This is probably best done with a smaller group of pupils or more collages prepared for a larger group.

Examples
- **Name ten objects beginning with the letter 'B'.**
- **Name six makes of car.**
- **Who is wearing a blue dress? (Show picture of the Queen.)**
- **What is the Alsatian doing? (Show picture of Alsatian jumping through a hoop.)**

How this could be varied and developed
Have a collection of magazines for participants to make up a 'surreal' collage. They could be given a theme.

Examples
- **sunny afternoon in the park**
- **nightmare**
- **the hurricane**

Guess the country

What to do
The teacher writes the names of ten countries on separate sheets of card and places these in different positions around the room. Participants form groups of four. The teacher calls out different cities from any of the countries, making some easy and others difficult. After the teacher calls each city, the groups decide which country they think the city is in and go to stand by the appropriate card. If they have made a correct guess they receive a point.

How this could be varied and developed
Participants remain in their groups. The teacher says a city and names a country to which the city belongs. If the groups believe the statement is true they remain standing; if they think it is false they sit down. They receive a point for each correct guess.

Examples
Rotterdam is in Holland – True   Dusseldorf is in Belguim – False

Match the adverts

What to do
The teacher collects a set of 20–30 illustrated magazine advertisements and cuts out the product and name from each advertisement. The named products are glued to

card and the illustrations to other pieces of card. Each illustration is given a number. Participants work in pairs and try to match the product with the illustration. They receive one point for each correct match.

It might help to have the products and illustrations attached to the walls around the room so pairs can spread out while looking at them.

How this could be varied and developed

Participants can discuss the objective of advertisements, e.g. What are they designed to achieve? How do they do this? Do they target different groups of people? How do they try to attract the right market group? Participants can work in pairs to produce an illustrated advertisement for a fictional product.

Missing pieces

What to do

In groups of 3–4 participants are given a simple jigsaw to complete. However one piece (or several according to group's ability) is incorrect, it belongs to another group's jigsaw. The groups must try to find their missing piece(s) and see which group can complete their puzzle first.

How this could be varied and developed

- Participants can discuss whether they like/dislike doing jigsaw puzzles.
- What kind of puzzle activities do they enjoy most and why? For example, crosswords, quizzes, mechanical puzzles.
- What is the point of puzzles? What skills do you learn when you do them?

Pairs quiz

What to do

Participants work in randomly chosen pairs. Each pair is given a prepared quiz paper on which to complete items.

Items can include
- putting a scribbled set of instructions in the correct order;
- 'spot the difference' pictures;
- unscrambling words from a list of ten (birds, countries etc.);
- find the odd man out;
- simple pictures to guess the phrases;
- matching (e.g. capitals to countries);
- sentences with vowels removed (e.g. bttr lt thn nvr – better late than never);
- how many 'S's in the following paragraph? Simon says his sister Susan is sure to sing at the summer solstice festival. She sings so sweetly says Simon so be sure you reserve some seats, so as not to miss seeing Susan.

How this could be varied and developed

The teacher gives each pair a different type of quiz question to devise in an allotted time of say, 5–10 minutes. Once they have devised one question, each pair is given a number according to the number of people in the group, e.g. in a group of 30, the pairs would be numbered 1–15. Each pair then lists 1–15 on a sheet of paper, putting in their own correct answer by their number. (If they were pair number 6, they would put the answer to their quiz question next to number 6.) Pairs then mingle and ask other pairs for their questions; they must write down an answer by the relevant number, before approaching a different pair. The first pair to have all the correct answers is the winner.

It is helpful if the pairs also put their answer next to the correct number on a master sheet held by the teacher, so that s/he can check off the answers to find the winning pair.

Picture stories

What to do
In small groups (3–4) participants 'tell a story' in a sequence of ten simple pictures. Pupils must try and make the pictures explicit and think about the 'information' they show. The pictures are then mixed up so the 'story' is not in the correct sequence. Groups swap 'stories' and try to put the pictures in the correct sequence and work out the story line.

How this could be varied and developed
Participants can discuss cartoon comic strips. What they like/dislike about them. What sort of characters would they choose to be the hero/heroine of a cartoon comic strip?

Treasure hunt

What to do
The participants work in pairs. Each pair has a prepared sheet of twenty clues. Displayed randomly around the room are twenty answers on cards. The participants walk around the room looking at the cards and noting the correct answers by each clue. The first pair to correctly match all the answers to the clues is the winner.

Example
- **This character wore boots in a well known children's story. Answer – Puss.**
- **Opponents will need these for a fight. Answer – boxing gloves.**
- **This brightens up every occasion. Answer – decorations.**

How this could be varied and developed
Divide the participants into two teams. Ask each team to devise twenty different clues and answers for the other team. One team member writes out the answers. The remaining team members write out the sets of clues so that there are enough for the other team to have one per pair (i.e. in a class of 28, the teams will have 14 pupils in each team so they will have to write out the clues seven times).

Teams have a race to see who can correctly complete the other's answers first.

Part IV
Theoretical background

19 Some theoretical background to Circle Time

Research has many times indicated the power of the group dynamic of Circle Time to effect change in pupils' behaviour, relationships, attitudes and learning (Mosley 1991, Mann 1995, Stevens 1995 and Tew 1998).

> The circle helps people to get to know you and find out how you feel.
>
> (Year 7 pupil, George Ward School, Melksham)

People ask, 'But where exactly did Circle Time originate?' – an impossible question to answer. The circle has been a symbol of unity, healing and power for thousands of years and many cultures have used the symbolic circle for problem-solving, discussion and goal achieving. The North American Indians, for example, used to sit in a circle with their talking object, often a feather or a pipe. Whoever was talking while holding the object would not have his train of thought interrupted by others in the circle.

In more recent times, Dr J. L. Moreno (1934, 1946) is the acknowledged forefather of all active groupwork approaches. While the UK has failed to explore the significance of his contribution to education, America has long acknowledged him as 'a great educator-therapist'. He has been, 'both directly, as well as indirectly through his students, a profound contributor to educational theory and practice and the pioneer of systematic training in human relationships' (Haas 1949: viii–ix).

It is Moreno's understanding of the importance of 'the group' and of the ways in which social interaction contributes to the development of self that makes his work so relevant to the debate as to why Circle Time has the power to affect the self-concept. Moreno viewed human beings as responsible for their own actions, and believed that their natural spontaneity and creativity could, through the medium of drama, free them to direct their lives in more satisfying ways. 'Spontaneity as a creative function endeavours to create the self and an adequate environment for it' (Moreno 1946: 101).

The model of Circle Time presented in this book draws heavily on a range of active learning approaches with their unique potential to encourage spontaneity, creativity, imagination, non-verbal communication, fun and reflection. The strategies have the potential to help pupils and teachers to understand their current situation and liberate them sufficiently to perceive new possibilities. A commitment to building self-esteem in the circle then develops the personal power needed to bring about the changes they wish to make.

> When we start our work in a circle I feel excited because I wonder what we are going to do.
>
> (Year 7 pupil, George Ward School, Melksham)

> I enjoyed Circle Time because it is taught in an interesting way. I think that it was really educational when things were acted out because I think it actually sunk into people's brains more.
> (Year 7 pupil, The Ridgeway School, Swindon)

The social interactionists

There are several important theoretical frameworks which inform why Circle Time strategies work. Some of the major contributions to our understanding come from humanistic psychology and social interactionist theory. The work of Mead (1934) and Cooley (1964) informed our understanding of the self-concept as a product of social interaction. As Circle Time is a social process, symbolic interactionist theory is of major relevance. It specifically describes the self as a social entity formed by the appraisal of others.

Cooley developed his idea of the 'looking-glass self' (1964). He came to believe that individuals and society are interdependent and that social acts and social norms modify each other. The individual's self-concept is a personalised construction of meaning, largely determined by what s/he believes others think of him/her. 'Each to each a looking glass, Reflects the other that doth pass' (Cooley 1964: 184).

We interact with others in a social context and they act as a mirror to us, a reflection of ourselves. We then subjectively interpret the reflection and from these perceived beliefs and evaluations we build our picture of ourselves.

> Circle Time does change you quite a lot when you talk about something. If you say 'I don't think that anyone likes me' and after the class someone says 'We do really like you but you are a bit quiet' or something like that, then it changes you.
> (Year 7 pupil, The Ridgeway School, Swindon)

Mead, a philosopher, sociologist and social psychologist, saw self-development as a social process facilitated by verbal and non-verbal communication. He agreed with Cooley's theory of the looking-glass self but went further, seeing the individual as interacting not only with others, but also with him/herself. The self is essentially reflexive. Every behaviour commences as an 'I' but develops and ends as a 'me' as it comes under the influence of societal constraints. 'I' provides the propulsion; 'me' provides direction (Burns 1982: 18).

Mead suggested that the behaviour of the individual can only be understood in terms of a social dynamic and therefore the individual act can only be comprehended as part of a whole. Circle Time strategies are designed to help individuals understand their behaviour and the response of other people towards it. It offers a model of helping that acknowledges that the behaviour of an individual pupil is embedded in the social interaction of his/her class group. It needs to be the class group that works with the pupil to help him/her become aware of the range of other responses available.

> I liked the teenage topic and health and hygiene too. In the teenage one, it made you think how you follow fashion because you want to be in with the crowd and you're afraid of being different. I liked passing the egg around and voicing our opinions. I thought it was cool how people had different opinions about different things.
> (Year 7 pupil, The Ridgeway School, Swindon)

Essential to Mead's contribution is the assertion that the self cannot be reorganised or reconstituted into a more positive one without altering the social relations of the self to others. Circle Time is bound by ground rules based on respect, valuing and reflecting back to participants a positive reflection of their selves. Their opinions are listened to, their contributions are acted upon, and their qualities and strengths are celebrated within a forum that will not tolerate any negativity or put-downs. Pupils experience themselves as creative agents within their own world. They have opportunities for initiating, reflecting and contributing. In other words, they are experiencing new opportunities for creating a different, more empathic, powerful and controlled self.

> Since I came to secondary school I like to know what people think of me and how they think of other people as well. I think the circle helped that because we moved about in the circle and did lots of circle games. Games are a good method of teaching us stuff and for getting to know other people.   (Year 7 pupil, The Ridgeway School, Swindon)

Further contributions of Humanistic Psychology

Humanistic psychology sees mankind as intrinsically good and each individual as positively motivated towards achieving his/her potential.

Maslow (1962) thought that psychology ought to concentrate on 'healthy' rather than ill people, on strengths and qualities rather than frailties and weaknesses. He described a hierarchy of human needs with physiological needs at its base and 'self-actualising' at the apex. His thesis was that if needs were met at each successive level of the hierarchy, from survival needs, through safety, to love, affection and belonging, then the individual would develop a positive self-image and finally be able to become what s/he had the potential to be.

Figure 19.1 shows how the physical act of sitting in a circle and the interaction that is produced by this format meets the successive levels of Maslow's hierarchy of needs. Certainly the pupils would concur with the view that Circle Time encourages more meaningful communication and builds confidence.

> If you sit in a circle you can see everyone, you can see them talking, you don't have to turn around and you can see them and hear them really well and you don't have anything to fiddle with so you concentrate more.

> I speak to people I wouldn't have spoken to before, or I wouldn't have said 'OK come and join our group' and things like that. I work with them more now.

> (Year 7 pupils, The Ridgeway School, Swindon)

Glasser (1965, 1969) developed his theory of Reality Therapy on ideas similar to Maslow. He saw all people as motivated to get love, social responsibility and self-worth, to be recognised and have a sense of power over life. All behaviour is viewed as an attempt to satisfy one of more of those needs and individuals are encouraged to replace actions which have produced self-destructive behaviour with new choices which lead to a more efficient need satisfaction. Both Maslow and Glasser saw a need to establish a sense of safety and belonging as a necessary precursor to building self-worth and bringing satisfaction.

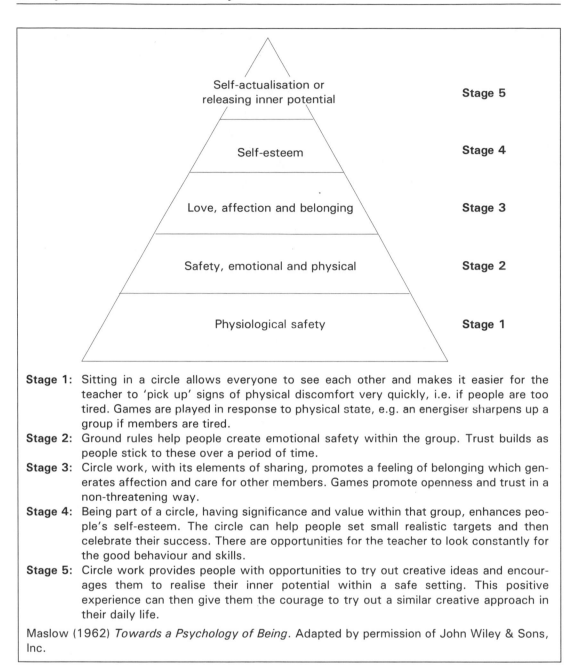

Stage 1: Sitting in a circle allows everyone to see each other and makes it easier for the teacher to 'pick up' signs of physical discomfort very quickly, i.e. if people are too tired. Games are played in response to physical state, e.g. an energiser sharpens up a group if members are tired.

Stage 2: Ground rules help people create emotional safety within the group. Trust builds as people stick to these over a period of time.

Stage 3: Circle work, with its elements of sharing, promotes a feeling of belonging which generates affection and care for other members. Games promote openness and trust in a non-threatening way.

Stage 4: Being part of a circle, having significance and value within that group, enhances people's self-esteem. The circle can help people set small realistic targets and then celebrate their success. There are opportunities for the teacher to look constantly for the good behaviour and skills.

Stage 5: Circle work provides people with opportunities to try out creative ideas and encourages them to realise their inner potential within a safe setting. This positive experience can then give them the courage to try out a similar creative approach in their daily life.

Maslow (1962) *Towards a Psychology of Being*. Adapted by permission of John Wiley & Sons, Inc.

Figure 19.1 Maslow's hierarchy of human needs and its application to circle work

> It makes you feel you are not the only person with problems and worries about yourself. It makes you have more self-confidence, more self-esteem because before I felt 'Oh I don't like my face or I wish I could change this.' But when you speak about things like that in the circle it makes you realise that other people have the same worries as you and you are not abnormal when you have those thoughts.
>
> (Year 7 pupil, The Ridgeway School, Swindon)

More recent theories and studies of the self-concept have been within the ambit of phenomenology, which LaBenne and Green (1969: 8) define as: 'the study of direct awareness'. Individual perception underpins phenomenology, based on the belief that 'man lives essentially in his own personal and subjective world' (Rogers 1959: 191).

Rogers (1951, 1961a, 1961b, 1970, 1983), while not discussing the origins of self-esteem directly, differentiated between the 'self' and the 'self-concept'. Self-concept comprises self-perceptions and the value attached to those perceptions. The self-concept is often incongruent with the organismic self because it is largely dependent on the attitudes and values of 'significant others'. The individual's perception is his/her reality and behaviour is in response to perception of an experience or situation. 'Phenomenology is concerned with a person's perception of reality not reality itself' (Burns 1979: 30).

Rogers's phenomenological framework is built on an understanding that self-concept is learned. An unhealthy self-conceptualisation with feelings of inferiority, inadequacy, failure, worthlessness and insecurity can therefore be unlearned or replaced, with learned feelings of worth, competence, adequacy and confidence. 'The individual has within him vast resources for self-understanding, for altering his self-concept, his attitudes, and his self-directed behaviour ... and that these resources can be tapped if only a definable climate of facilitative psychological attitudes can be provided' Rogers (1974: 15).

The core attitudes Rogers saw as necessary to facilitate change in the self-concept were warmth, respect and acceptance, especially from those who are significant 'others' in the life of the individual.

> When we go into a circle I look forward to it – it gets us quite sort of close.
> (Year 7 pupil, George Ward School, Melksham)

> I think sitting in a circle helps people to feel good about themselves and express their feelings. (Year 7 pupil, George Ward School, Melksham)

> I feel happy in the circle because I know I can say anything and people will not laugh at me. (Year 7 pupil, George Ward School, Melksham)

The role of the peer group

Cooley (1964) and Rogers (1951) both used the term 'significant others' to mean those persons who are important or who have significance in the development of self-concept. Parents or caregivers are usually the most significant 'others' in a child's life because they have the greatest contact and are most likely to intensify or reduce feelings of insecurity, helplessness, or sense of worth.

Brim (1965, cited in Coleman 1974) carried out research that showed motivation is generated by interpersonal relationships. How good or bad a person feels depends on the degree to which s/he lives up to the expectations of other people. The significance of the other person affects the strength of influence. As the child grows, the range of reference figures increases. Studies by Kirchner and Vondraek (1975, cited in Burns 1979: 162) suggest that

> the peer-group influence becomes increasingly important as adolescence progresses, hitting a peak at around the years of middle adolescence. The self-concept continues to change as the expanding social environment influences it. The child has an increased sensitivity to the approval and disapproval of peers and teachers because they will like and accept him/her for what s/he is, not out of a sense of duty.

Feedback from teachers and peers

Feedback in the form of verbal and non-verbal communication provides the evidence which informs observations and evaluations about oneself. If adult and peer relationships provide acceptance and opportunities for feeling worthwhile and responsible, a child will gain a successful identity (Glasser 1965). Success brings a sense of competence and motivation to succeed increases. On the other hand, the person who does not gain love and self-worth through experiencing success will become angry, frustrated, hostile and aggressive. They will try to meet their needs by force using attention-seeking, aggressive and hostile tactics, or by becoming withdrawn, alienated and isolated.

Feedback from significant others is important in modifying self-concept because it contains others' definitions and expectations of us. We tend readily to accept their judgements and so come to behave in accordance with those definitions. This process is in effect a self-fulfilling prophecy (Rosenthal and Jacobson 1968). Beynon (1985) studied initial encounters between pupils and staff in a secondary school and demonstrated how easily and how early 'labelling' of pupils can take place. Once established, these 'labels' can be extremely difficult to challenge or alter.

Burns (1982) demonstrated that if pupils are offered respectful relationships and a warm supportive ethos their social and academic performance will flourish. In Circle Time, security in the group is built so that it becomes a place of trust and feeling valued. If this group always attends to the individual, invites him/her to share in fun games and applauds successes, then the individual begins to see him/herself as a stronger more worthwhile and valued person. The group reflects back to the individual a positive mirror of themselves. Cooley (1964) called this reflection 'the looking-glass self'. He, like Mead, argued that a person's self-concept grows out of his or her social interactions. So if the group reflects a positive image, the individual begins to 'take on' these attitudes.

> If someone says thank you to you, it makes you sort of like them more. You feel like you've helped them. You wouldn't usually go up to someone and say 'Thank you for being my friend' but if you say it in the circle it makes you feel happy.
>
> (Year 7 pupil, The Ridgeway School, Swindon)

More recently theorists such as Bandura (1977) and Michenbaum (1977) have proposed a social learning theory that takes into account the importance of internal events and thought processes in shaping behaviour. They have stressed that observational learning or modelling plus enactment is a powerful form of learning. In Circle Time, pupils are given opportunities to watch and reflect as their peers and their teachers enact a process based on respect. They observe role-plays where they and their peers try out different, calmer responses to bullying, persuasion or harassment.

Emotional intelligence

In the past 15 years there has been a wealth of research on human intelligence and learning. Perhaps the most exciting work in terms of the implications for education is that of Howard Gardner (1984, 1991 and 1993). He has highlighted how narrow the

Western interpretation of intelligence has become. In our education systems we rely heavily on logical and linguistic methods for assessing progress and attributing prowess. Yet Gardner's work has called our previous assumptions into question and schools may well have to consider a wider range of 'intelligences' in the pupils of the future.

Of particular relevance to Circle Time is the work of Daniel Goleman (1996). He has considered aspects of Gardner's work and focused on the range of skills that make up 'emotional intelligence'. Emotional intelligence underpins the notion of democracy with its respect for people and property. The ability to manage feelings in oneself and other people and the capacity for empathy lead directly to a more tolerant attitude to others and a greater respect for difference. The skills that Goleman sees as making up emotional intelligence include:

- **Knowing one's emotions – self-awareness, recognising feelings and the ability to monitor them – important in decision making and valuing one's own decisions.**
- **Managing emotions – handling feelings so they are appropriate – necessary for dealing effectively with the setbacks of life.**
- **Motivating oneself – marshalling emotions in the service of a goal – essential for paying attention, mastery, creativity and stifling impulsiveness.**
- **Recognising emotions in others – empathy, a fundamental 'people skill' – necessary for the caring professions.**
- **Handling relationships – the skill of managing emotions in others – renders it possible to interact smoothly with others.** **(Goleman 1996: 43)**

Goleman argues that social intelligence as distinct from academic learning is a key part of what makes people do well in the practicalities of life. Mentally healthy and capable adults have a mixture of intellectual and emotional acuity.

In conclusion

Teachers are charged with the task of educating individuals 'to think and act for themselves, with an acceptable set of personal qualities and values which also meet the wider social demands of adult life.' (National Curriculum Council: The Whole Curriculum 1991a: 7). More and more we need strategies to actively encourage personal and social development.

Through the years,[1] regular Circle Time has been shown to be powerfully effective in helping to:

- **build friendships;**
- **create trust;**
- **eliminate put-downs;**
- **promote personal and collective responsibility;**
- **encourage self-discipline;**
- **improve listening skills;**
- **promote better behaviour;**
- **develop personal integrity;**
- **develop empathy;**
- **create a sense of belonging;**
- **teach assertive skills;**
- **solve problems;**
- **promote understanding;**
- **improve relationships;**
- **integrate all special-needs pupils with the whole class.**

141

So much of the work has been carried out in the primary sector. Secondary schools also need to invest in programmes that offer young people a chance to relax away from academic pressures in a forum where each person is potentially as talented as the next in the field of human relationships.[2] As Burns summed up in his wide-ranging review of self-concept, programmes that 'guide pupils and teachers towards a better understanding of themselves and their interpersonal relationships are rare' (Burns 1979: 310). It is exciting to report that twenty years later such a programme is already flourishing in thousands of primary schools and is beginning to be adopted in the secondary sector.

Notes

1. Mann, C. (1995), Stevens, V. (1995), Tew, M. (1998), Dawson et al. (1998), Scottish Home Office.
2. This year, The Calouste Gulbenkian Foundation sponsored some independently evaluated research into using Quality Circle Time with year 7 in The Headlands School, Swindon. A report is being prepared for the Calouste Gulbenkian and will be available in the autumn.

Appendices

A: Checklist to see if I am a good listening role model

Reflect on whether you offer each pupil a positive, valuing relationship by looking through the following statements:

- Do I genuinely like all the pupils in my tutor group/class?
- Do I really care about each pupil?
- Can I find something good to think/say about each pupil?
- Do I speak respectfully to each individual?
- Am I able to avoid confrontation?
- Do I regularly give positive feedback to each pupil on his or her positive attributes?
- Am I able to forgive each pupil?
- Do I expect certain pupils to behave badly?
- Do I assume certain pupils are guilty before listening to the facts?
- Am I able to apologise to pupils if I have reacted unjustly?
- Is my body language consistent with my words when I speak to pupils? For example, do I ask them how they are getting on but look 'poised to rush off'?
- Do my tutor times/PSE lessons ensure that every pupil will eventually achieve a moment of success which I then take time to notice?

B: Inventory of behaviours of children at risk of disaffection

Do you have any pupil in your year 7 or 8 teaching group who regularly causes you some concern? If so, please put the pupil's name in the box and then tick the behaviours that are most often shown by this pupil. These are only pointers. We have left clear boxes for you to fill in your own observations.

Many thanks. We hope this will help us to choose the right pupils to join a proposed support group.

Name of pupil	
Name of teacher	

A. Behaviour characterised by lack of self control	
1. Often arrives late with excuses about forgetting which lesson it was, or having returned to previous lesson to find some lost possessions	
2. During lessons calls out loudly and repeatedly. Often puts up hand without knowing the answer - or even remembering the question	
3. Rarely has the appropriate equipment	
4. Cannot concentrate when given verbal or written instructions – will ask questions immediately	
5. After a short attempt at task becomes very restless and fidgety	
6. When questioned about that task has forgotten its initial purpose	
7. Is unable to work independently or make balanced decisions at any time	
8. Physically clumsy	
9. Actively distracts others from their work	
10.	
11.	
B. Withdrawn behaviour	
1. Will sit alone or else has to be 'put beside' partner	
2. Never volunteers information, puts up hand or asks for clarification	
3. If directly questioned, looks embarrassed, may blush or fidget	
4. Rarely smiles	
5. Will often be the focus of other pupils' derisory or uncomplimentary comments	
6. Body posture is often stooped or awkward in movement	
7. Is seen to be isolated in playground or walking around the school	
8. Occasionally absent from sessions	
9. Often eyes are downcast. Is unable to sustain eye contact with others	
10.	
11.	
C. Hostile behaviour	
1. Rarely shows interest in content of lesson or its related discussions	
2. When questioned, will either look away from teacher in bored or calculated insolence – or else will stare directly with a challenging aggressive stance	
3. Will always sit away or turn back towards you if given the opportunity	
4. Will never initiate a conversation with an adult unless it is related to the pupil's feeling of having been unfairly treated, pupil's boredom or any other topic that elicits his/her contempt	

5. Deliberately attempts to stop lesson's progress, or conversely will express alienation by complete lack of attention, arriving very late or not at all!	
6. Occasional burst of aggressive behaviour, either towards the teacher or peers	
7. Deliberated destruction or vandalism of school property	
8. Actively distracts others in a deliberate attempt to disrupt lessons	

C: Survey for senior managers

- How long is the lunchtime period?
- How long is the morning break?
- How long is the afternoon break? (if relevant)
- Have you ever held any INSET for teaching staff on the organisation/management of lunchtimes?
- Have you ever held any INSET for midday supervisory assistants on the organisation/management of lunchtimes?
- Have you ever held any INSET for midday supervisory assistants and teaching staff together on the organisation/management of lunchtimes?
- Have you devised any lunchtime reward systems for midday supervisory assistants to use?
- What sanctions systems have you agreed with your midday supervisory assistants?
- Do any of your management policies mention lunchtime supervision?
- In which policies are your lunchtime rules included? Who receives copies? Where are they displayed?
- Do you discuss with or communicate with parents about: a) Lunchtime arrangements? b) Eating policies/healthy eating?
- Do you offer any activities/clubs at lunchtimes?
- Do you have regular meetings with midday supervisory assistants? If so, who else attends these meetings and to whom is any relevant feedback given?
- Do midday supervisory assistants in your school receive any induction training?
- Do midday supervisory assistants in your school receive a written list of procedures?
- Do midday supervisory assistants in your school receive feedback after any lunchtime incidents?
- Does your school have any security procedures for visitors?
- Are pupils allowed to go off-site during lunchtimes? If so, what criteria are used to warrant this privilege?
- Are there any arrangements (other than detention) for known trouble-makers at lunchtimes?
- Have you ever had a fire drill at lunchtime?
- Have the midday supervisory assistants received information about fire drill arrangements?
- Is there anything you have done recently to improve lunchtimes?
- Is there anything you have done recently to improve the dining hall system?
- Have the catering staff in your school ever had their views surveyed about the problems of lunchtimes?
- Have you had any drug related incidents in your school during the last year? If so, did they occur during the lunchtime period?

Bibliography

Ayers, H., Clarke, D. and Murray, A. (1995) *Perspectives on Behaviour*. London: David Fulton Publishers.

Bandura, A. (1977) *Social Learning Theory*. New York: Prentice Hall.

Bandura, A. (1997) *Self-Efficacy: The Exercise of Control*. New York: W. H. Freeman.

Bateson, G. (1979) *Mind and Nature: A Necessary Unity*. New York: Dutton.

Beynon, J. (1985) *Initial Encounters in the Secondary School*. London: Falmer Press.

Burns, R. (1979) *The Self Concept*. London: Longman.

Burns, R. (1982) *Self-Concept Development and Education*. Eastbourne: Holt, Rinehart & Winston.

Coleman, J. C. (1974) *Relationships in Adolescence*. London: Routledge & Kegan Paul.

Coleman, J. C. (1980) *The Nature of Adolescence*. London: Methuen.

Cooley, C. H. (1964) *Human Nature and the Social Order*. New York: Schocken Books.

Cooper, P., Smith, C. J. and Upton, G. (1994) *Emotional and Behavioural Difficulties: Theory to Practice*. London: Routledge.

Cooper, P. and Upton, G. (1990) 'An ecosystemic approach to emotional and behavioural difficulties in school', *Educational Psychology* 10(4), 301–19.

Daniels, H. *et al*. (1999) *Emotional and Behavioural Difficulties in Mainstream Schools*. London: HMSO.

Dawson, N. and McNess, E. (1998) A report on the use of Circle Time in Wiltshire primary schools, University of Bristol, Graduate School of Education.

De Shazer, S. (1982) *Patterns of Brief Family Therapy*. New York: Guiford Press.

De Shazer, S. (1985) *Keys to Solutions in Brief Therapy*. New York: W. W. Norton.

DfEE (1998) *Excellence for All Children: Meeting Special Educational Needs*. London: DfEE.

DfEE (1999) *Social Inclusion: Pupil Support: draft guidance*. London: DfEE.

Durrant, M. (1995) *Creative Strategies for School Problems*. USA: W. W. Norton.

Elton, Lord (1989) *Discipline in Schools: Report of Committee of Enquiry Chaired by Lord Elton*. London: HMSO.

Eurest (1997) *The Eurest Lunchtime Report*. London: Compass Group UK Division.

Gardner, H. (1984) *Frames of Mind*. Heinemann.

Gardner, H. (1991) *The Unschooled Mind: How Children Think and How Schools should Teach*. London: Fontana Press.

Gardner, H. (1993a) *Frames of Mind: The Theory of Multiple Intelligences*. 2nd edn. London: Fontana Press.

Gardner, H. (1993b) *Multiple Intelligences: The Theory in Practice*. London: Basic Books.

Glasser, W. (1965) *Reality Therapy*. New York, Harper & Row.

Glasser, W. (1969) *Schools without Failure*. New York: Harper Crompton Books.

Goleman, D. (1996) *Emotional Intelligence*. London: Bloomsbury.

Greenhalgh, P. (1991) 'Working with groups: the functions of the group in work with children experiencing emotional and behavioural difficulties', *Maladjustment and Therapeutic Education* 9(1), 28–33.

Greenhalgh, P. (1994) *Emotional Growth and Learning*. London: Routledge.

Haas, R. (1949) *Psychodrama and Sociodrama in American Education*. New York: Beacon House.

Hanko, G. (1985) *Special Needs in Ordinary Classrooms*. Oxford: Basil Blackwell.

Hanko, G. (1999) *Increasing Competence Through Collaboration*. London: David Fulton Publishers.

Hopson, B. and Scally, M. (1981) *Lifeskills Teaching*. London: McGraw Hill.

Katz, A. (1999) *Leading Lads*. Research sponsored by TOPMAN. Oxford: Oxford University Press.

LaBenne, W. D. and Green, A. I. (1969) *Educational Implications of Self-Concept Theory*. California: Goodyear.

Lawrence, D. (1973) *Improving Reading Through Counselling*. London: Ward Lock.

Lawrence, D. (1985) 'Improving reading and self-esteem', *Educational Research* **27**(3), 194–200.

Lawrence, D. (1988) *Enhancing Self-Esteem in the Classroom*. London: Paul Chapman.

Lefcourt, H. M. (1982) *Locus of Control*. New Jersey: Lawrence Erlbaum Associates.

Mann, C. (1995) *Developing Children's Self-esteem through Thinking Skills in a Supportive Group Setting*. Unpublished M.Ed. dissertation, Bristol University.

Maslow, A. (1962) *Towards a Psychology of Being*. New York: Van Nostrand Reinhold.

Mead, G. H. (1934) *Mind, Self and Society*. Chicago: University of Chicago.

Michenbaum, D. (1977) *Cognitive Behaviour Modification*. New York: Plenum Press.

Minuchin, S. (1974) *Families and Family Therapy*. London: Tavistock.

Molnar, A. and Lindquist, B. (1989) *Changing Problem Behaviour in schools*. San Francisco: Jossey-Bass.

Moreno, J. L. (1934) *Who Shall Survive?* New York: Beacon House.

Moreno, J. L. (1946) *Psychodrama*, 2nd revised edn. New York: Beacon House.

Moreno, J. L. (1959) *Psychodrama* Vol. 2, Foundations of Psychotherapy. New York: Beacon House.

Moreno, J. L. (1994) *Sociodrama: A Method for the Analysis of Social Conflicts*, Psychodrama Monographs, No. 1. New York: Beacon House.

Mosley, J. (1988) Some implications arising from a small scale study of a circle based programme initiated for the tutorial period, *Pastoral Care* **6**(2).

Mosley, J. (1989) *Circletime*. Trowbridge: Wiltshire, Positive Press.

Mosley, J. (1991a) *All Round Success – A Practical Guide to Enhancing Self-esteem in the Primary Classroom*. Wiltshire Education Authority.

Mosley, J. (1991b) An evaluative account of the working of a dramatherapy peer support group within a comprehensive school. *Support for Learning* **6**(4), 156–64.

Mosley, J. (1993) *Turn Your School Round*. Cambridge: LDA.

Mosley, J. (1996) *Quality Circle Time*. Cambridge: LDA.

Mosley, J (1999) *More Quality Circle Time*. Cambridge: LDA.

Mosley, J. and Gillibrand, E. (1995) *She Who Dares Wins*. London: HarperCollins.

OFSTED (1995) *Framework for the Inspection of Nursery, Primary, Middle, Secondary and Special Schools*. London: HMSO.

Rogers, C. (1951) *Client-centred Therapy*. London: Constable.

Rogers, C. (1959) 'A theory of therapy, personality, and interpersonal relationships as developed in a client centred framework'. In Koch, S. (ed.), *Psychology: A Study of Science*. New York: McGraw Hill.

Rogers, C. (1961a) *On Becoming a Person*. Boston: Houghton Mifflin.

Rogers, C. (1961b) *A Way of Being*. Boston: Houghton Mifflin.

Rogers, C. (1970) *Carl Rogers in Encounter Groups*. New York: Harper & Row.

Rogers, C. (1983) *Freedom to Learn for the 80s*. Merril: Macmillan.

Rosenthal, R. and Jacobson, L. (1968) *Pygmalion in the Classroom*. New York: Rinehart & Winston.

Rotter, J. B. (1966) 'Generalised expectancies for internal versus external control of reinforcement', *Psychol. Monogr.* **80**(609).

Selvini-Palazzoni, M. (1978) *Paradox and Counter Paradox*. New York: Jason Aronson.

Stevens, V. (1995) *Self-esteem, Circle Time and Children with Literacy Difficulties*. Unpublished dissertation, Bristol University.

Taylor, M. (1998) *Values Education and Values in Education: A Guide to the Issues Commission by ATL*. London: NFER.

Tew, M. (1998) 'Circle Time – a much neglected resource in secondary schools', *Pastoral Care in Education*, **16**(3).

Tew, M. (1998) *Using Circle Time in Personal and Social Education*, unpublished M.Ed. dissertation, Bristol University.

Von Bertalanffy, L. (1969) *General System Theory: Foundations, Development, Applications*. New York: George Brazillier.

Watkins, C. (1997) *Managing Classroom Behaviour*. London: Association of Teachers and Lecturers (ATL).

Resources

Training for your staff

The Jenny Mosley Consultancies have well trained consultants, experienced in all aspects of the Whole School Quality Circle Time Model, who are available to visit your work-place to give courses and workshops to all your teaching and support staff.

- **On a *Closure Day*, all staff, teachers, lunchtime supervisors, ancillary and administration staff are invited to participate in a day that focuses on all aspects of the model, including teambuilding, developing positive ethos and valuing individuals.**
- **On an *In-School Day*, the school does not close and a Circle Time approach is demonstrated with whole classes of pupils observed by a range of staff. In addition, Circle Time meetings are held for lunchtime supervisors and an Action Plan for the shool is drawn up with key members of staff.**

Training for the Trainers

Our research and experience have revealed that one reason the model can become diluted or vulnerable is because there are people who give courses based on our model, yet they themselves have never attended any of our in-depth courses. They have either attended a one-day course, or are working merely from using our books. Jenny Mosley runs week-long in-depth courses and then issues accompanying certificates. These courses are held nationally.

For details of the above, or requests for any further information, please contact:

Jenny Mosley Consultancies
8 Westbourne Road
Trowbridge
Wiltshire, BA14 0AJ

Tel: 01225 767157; Fax: 01225 755631

Email: circletime@jennymosley.demon.co.uk

Website: www.jennymosley.demon.co.uk

Index